Kingdom Culture School of Ministry Core

By Kristen D'Arpa

Kingdom Culture School of Ministry

Copyright ©2016 by Kristen D'Arpa
Third Edition Revised 2020
All rights reserved
ISBN 9781530789603

This book is protected by the copyright law of the United States of America. No part of this book may be reproduced or transmitted in any form or by any means, electronic or mechanical, including photocopying, recording or by any information storage and retrieval system, without written permission from the author, except for the inclusion of brief quotations in a review.

Unless otherwise noted, all Scripture quotations are from the Holy Bible, New King James Version. Copyright © 1982 by Thomas Nelson, Inc. Used by permission. All rights reserved.

Scripture quotations marked (NLT) are taken from the Holy Bible, New Living Translation, copyright ©1996, 2004, 2007, 2013, 2015 by Tyndale House Foundation. Used by permission of Tyndale House Publishers, Inc., Carol Stream, Illinois 60188. All rights reserved.

Scripture quotations marked (NASB) are taken from the Holy Bible, NEW AMERICAN STANDARD BIBLE®, Copyright © 1960,1962,1963,1968,1971,1972,1973,1975,1977,1995 by The Lockman Foundation. Used by permission.

Scripture quotations marked (NIV) are taken from THE HOLY BIBLE, NEW INTERNATIONAL VERSION®, NIV® Copyright © 1973, 1978, 1984, 2011 by Biblica, Inc.® Used by permission. All rights reserved worldwide.

Scripture quotations marked (TPT) are from The Passion Translation®. Copyright © 2017, 2018 by Passion & Fire Ministries, Inc. Used by permission. All rights reserved. ThePassionTranslation.com.

For more information about other school manuals, live-taught schools, and online schools go to:

KristenDArpa.com

What Others are Saying About Kristen D'Arpa and Kingdom Culture School of Ministry

I am very excited to see believers across the planet being trained, equipped, and activated to see the kingdom of heaven come to earth. There is a company of people that are responding to the heart of God to see humanity touched by His power and love. This curriculum is another one of those pieces of the puzzle to help see this take place in our lifetime. **I encourage those who are hungry to learn, grow, and be activated to take a look at this manual. Enjoy!**

Eric Johnson
Senior Pastor, Bethel Church, Redding, CA
Author of *Momentum* and *Christ in You*

This training manual is a powerful and extensive tool to renew the mind with kingdom thinking and activate you into kingdom living. Much of what God has promised us is already accessible, we just need to learn how to take hold of it, and this manual teaches you how. It has an easy to use format that makes it accessible to anyone wanting to grow in a supernatural lifestyle. **In the hands of those hungry for more of God, this manual will be a catalyst for revival.**

Steve Backlund
Founder of Igniting Hope Ministries
Senior Associate Leader, Bethel Leaders Network

One of the greatest challenges in our generation is the passiveness of believers who spend years attending church and accumulating head knowledge that is hardly ever put into practice. **The *Kingdom Culture School of Ministry* pushes Christians from religious inertia into Holy Spirit action by releasing them into an adventurous faith-building, life-changing, and God-glorifying kingdom adventure.** I love it!

Evangelist Rubens Cunha
International Healing Evangelist and Founder of Global Gospel Action, Brazil

---

The *Kingdom Culture School of Ministry* is a powerful tool for people of all ages who desire to learn to be used of God in a powerful way to release the kingdom of heaven every day of their lives, in all circumstances. This is done so profoundly by reading, understanding, and applying simple Gospel truths that Kristen has put together in her *Kingdom Culture* books. The information found in these books has been compiled from years of active involvement in life-changing ministries and schools of ministry from all over the world. **If you desire to have miracles, signs, and wonders flow through your life, and if you are longing to gain a clear understanding of who you are in Christ and what God says about you, then the *Kingdom Culture School of Ministry* is for you.**

Dave Hauer
International Crusade Director who's been a part of seeing over 13 million people come to Jesus
Pastoral Elder, The House Church

Kristen has produced three manuals that help teachers and students to spread revival. Kristen has captured the Lord's heart that we walk in abundant life and feed His sheep. The activation component in each lesson helps the learner strengthen their skills by risking and applying what they have learned. **It is a tool that produces disciples of nations.** Kristen has been able to distill revival teaching and make the lessons user-friendly and practical. **These manuals help the reader step right in the middle of the 1 billion soul harvest as effective ministers of the Gospel. These manuals can be used at any seminary and in refugee camps and orphanages.** Kristen's manuals are equipping students and leaders to display Jesus as the Desire of Nations.

Anne Kalvestrand
Director of the Art of Peace Institute, which acts for peace in the Middle East
Missionary, Researcher, Former State Department Senior Fellow with an extensive background in Bahrain, China, Mongolia, Israel, Egypt, Kuwait, Qatar, Ethiopia, Iraq, Syria, Turkey, and Dubai

---

The *Kingdom Culture School of Ministry* manual has so many tools for believers to learn about identity, ways to evangelize, and creative ways to hear from God and then bring God's core values and lifestyle into our everyday life! **If you want to see the fulfillment of your supernatural potential, I would highly recommend this manual!**

Theresa Dedmon
Creative Arts Director, BSSM and Bethel Church, Redding, CA

Across the globe God is on the move. We hear of great exploits and breakthroughs wrought by God's children who are living testaments to the declaration, "Let Your kingdom come, let Your will be done on earth as it is in heaven." In these amazing times of heaven's invasion of the earthly realm, there's a great need for the body of Christ to not just go after breakthroughs, but to take territories for the King and establish kingdom culture. It is culture that sustains and expands the move of God.

As the Holy Spirit progressively stirs up divine hunger in the hearts of God's children for more, there's a need for effective tools and trainings that will equip the believers in intentionally building a culture that would host heaven. There are emerging leaders who have learned to walk the path of honor and have served spiritual leaders and fathers who in turn, imparted to them spiritual inheritance and wisdom. These leaders are anointed and graced to equip the believers to walk in their identity and authority as children of the King. The author of this training manual is one of them.

Kristen D'Arpa has walked the path and the process of becoming a daughter of God. I am a witness that *Kingdom Culture School of Ministry* is more than just a training module for her, she has lived life as a lover of God, freely giving what she has received in the secret place. **The *Kingdom Culture School of Ministry* is valuable for individuals, leaders, and movements who are hungry to co-labor with God in transforming the earth with heaven's reality. I highly recommend this God-breathed training to all.**

Paul Yadao
Destiny Ministries International, Philippines
Pastor, Author, and Speaker

This is an amazing approach to the age old problem of how the church can pull the future age (the kingdom of God) into everyday life and reality (1 Thessalonians 1:5). **This study was the single most helpful thing I have seen or been a part of in my whole church experience.** I had a "taste and see that the Lord is good" experience while reading it (Psalm 34:8).

Dr. Doyal VanGelder
Pastor, Missionary, and Church Planter

This material is, hands down, the best, most concise ministry training I've ever seen. It's clear, powerful, and best of all, based entirely on getting people to do supernatural ministry from supernatural mindsets. **It's impossible to go through this training without understanding more of who God says you are, seeing people healed, releasing destiny through prophetic words, and knowing how to make the supernatural a normal part of everyday life.** It's personally impacted my family and helped turn my 8-year-old daughter into a prophesying machine. I can't recommend this enough!

Nathanael White
Senior Pastor, Presence Church
Author of *Become You*

Kristen D'Arpa's *Kingdom Culture School of Ministry* manuals are treasures of wisdom, forged in experience, and distilled in clear language by a very anointed and godly young woman. Wherever we are in our walk with God—newly reborn or seasoned believer—we can benefit from the many truths set forth in this manual. **It's versatile and can be so useful for group or personal study. So much is contained in these pages—even activation activities, to allow the reader to practice what is being learned. Going through these manuals will be a transformative experience.** I highly recommend them and their author.

Pam Spinosi
International Student Liaison, BSSM and Testimony Writer, Bethel Church, Redding, CA

Kingdom Culture School of Ministry is so fantastic for so many people! We have used it in our classes in Bible School in Poland, Belarus, and the States and in seminars with multi-level age groups. The practicality of bringing the kingdom directly into lives with immediate application through the activations has been amazing. One of our translators said after the activation from The Old Man is Dead, **"I finally get it!" People are set free; Scripture pierces their hearts and there is immediate change. People love the interactions with each other over simple concepts that are suddenly born into life in them. Such fun!** We are excited that it is being translated into Polish, and our Belarussian people said they wanted it done immediately in Russian as well.

Roger and Myrna Eilers
Founder of Ram's Horn Ministry, Former Directors of Christ for the Nations, Poland
Missionaries to Eastern Europe for 25+ years

Kristen D'Arpa is the real deal. She lives and breathes the truths within this book. This is not a collection of concepts to her, it is a lifestyle she has embraced and walks out in her daily life. It is an absolute gift to the body of Christ to have her heart and passion for the kingdom of God spilled out for all of us in the pages of this book. Not only can we whole-heartedly endorse the content of this book, but we can whole-heartedly endorse the woman from whose heart it poured! **This concise and easy to use book provides the perfect starting point for teaching and training your children all about what it means to be a son or daughter in His kingdom!**

Jonathan and Amy Claussen
Founders of GoFam Ministries
Author of *Restoring the Power of Family*

Dedication

To Mom and Dad

I would not be who I am or where I am without you.

Your love, support, and encouragement have been my foundation for many years.

Thank you for so wisely stewarding the heritage of faith that runs so deeply throughout our

family line. You've truly allowed your ceiling to become my floor.

All that I have is yours. May the fruit of this work

be a blessing and a crown to you.

All my love!

- Kristen

Table of Contents

Foreword	i
A Word from the Author	iii

Introduction — 1

Identity — 13

God is Good	14
God Only Does Good Things	15
Made in God's Image	16
Loved, and Loving	17
Connecting with the Lord	18
My Old Self is Gone, and I am New	19
Adopted Into the Family	20
Be	22

Kingdom Mindsets — 23

Kingdom Generosity	24
Honor	25
Serve Others	26
Connection in Relationships	27
Generational Thinking	28
Rest	29
Ministering the Presence of the Lord	30
Impartation	31
On Earth as it is in Heaven	32
Declarations	33
The Power of the Testimony	34
What We Focus on We Empower	35
Peace Beyond Understanding	36
Strengthen Yourself in the Lord	37
Spiritual Warfare	38
Jesus is the Most Normal Christian . . .	39
The Light is Green Unless It's Red	40

The Bible — 41

Relationship with the Author	42
Connecting with the Bible (SOAP)	43
The Three Crosses	44
Bible Study	46
Pray the Bible	47
Biblical Meditation	48
Creative Bible Studies	49

Foundational Principles — 51

Repentance	52
Water Baptism	53
Local Church	54
Giving	55
Communion	56
Laying on of Hands	57
Praise and Worship	58

Personal Health — 59

Forgiveness	60
Release Mercy, and Forgive Sins	61
Release and Receive	62
Finding the Root	63
Healthy Living	64

Outreach — 65

Fear Not	66
Connect	67
How Can I Pray for You?	68
Feeling God's Presence	69
Your Salvation Testimony	70
Sharing the Gospel	72

Prayer For Salvation	74
Four Ways to Grow	76
Discipleship	78
Treasure Hunts	80
Relational Outreach	82

Spiritual Gifts 83
Holy Spirit Baptism	84
Tongues	85
Word of Knowledge	86
Discerning of Spirits	87
Word of Wisdom	88

Physical Healing 89
Five Step Healing Model	90
Words of Knowledge for Healing	91
Additional Healing Activations	92

Prophecy 93
Ways God Speaks	94
Strengthen, Encourage, and Comfort	95
Name-Based Prophecies	96
Image-Based Prophecies	97
It's All About Love	98
Processing Prophecy	99
Rapid Fire Prophecy	100
Hearing from God, Prophecy, and ...	101
A Skit About the Role of the Holy Spirit ...	104

Kingdom Creativity 109
Creative Identity	110
Creative Problem Solving	111

Societal Transformation 113
Adam and Eve: Having Dominion	114
Abraham: Seeking Mercy	115
Joseph: Solutions to Problems	116
Solomon: Wisdom in the Details	117
The Seven Mountains of Society	118
Prayer Evangelism	119
Pray for and Honor Leaders	120
Two Ways to See the World	121
Traditional Christian Worldview	122
Kingdom Worldview	123
Equipped and Equipping	124
Change the World, Start at Home	125
Scriptural Background for the Kingdom ...	126

Facilitator's Guide 127
Being a Kingdom Culture Facilitator	128
How to Facilitate a Kingdom Group	129
Setting Up Your Group	132
Possible Group Structure	133
Shorter Course Options	134
Ministry Tunnel 101	136

Additional Information 137
How it All Began	138
Acknowledgements	141
Kingdom Culture School Resources	143

Foreword

My wife and I planted our church in April of 2006. Our heads were full of dreams for all that God was going to do. Both of us had grown up in the church, so we had preconceived ideas of what it was supposed to look like. Our hearts longed to be in fellowship with other believers hungering for God's kingdom and we wanted to see the work of Jesus touching lives. The question was, "How do you create that?"

I had come to Jesus during a revival service in 1997 where I encountered the Lord's presence in such a real and tangible way. His power transformed my life and I wanted that for others. In my heart I pictured a church where every gathering buzzed with people praying and ministering to one another. Healings and miracles would happen regularly. The air would be filled with worship and testimonies of God working in power through the lives of believers. I could see it so clearly in my heart.

The problem was that I did not have a clear pathway to get us there. I would daydream about all that God was going to do through our ministry, but when the daydream ended, I was still setting up a portable PA system in a hotel ballroom. The distance between our humble beginnings and what God had put in my heart seemed worlds apart.

I sought the wisdom of other leaders and attended church planting events for inspiration. I read up on the trending and relevant church planting models and even tried to join networks that seemed to know what they were doing. Unfortunately, every model of church ministry we were hearing about had a different vision than the one I could see in my heart. We were going to have to pioneer our own way.

I felt like God had put a unique calling on our church that was specific to our region and people. As it turns out, I am not alone. God has put a unique calling on every church. So while I could learn from other churches, copying what someone else did wasn't going to produce the fruit we were called to produce. We had our own identity and unique calling.

What was on my heart was to see each person in my congregation fully equipped with ministry tools that were usable in real life situations. The business executive and the single mom should both have skills to release the kingdom in their respective worlds. We had people from every walk of life attending church services, so creating this kind of engagement was going to take an intentional process. We had to be deliberate in our approach to forming values and culture, but we still needed a clear process for activating ministry tools.

Right in the middle of this formation season, the Lord brought Kristen D'Arpa to us. She was a gift from God to our community. Her passion as a revivalist was mixed beautifully with the strengths of administration. She jumped into church life and worked hard to empower our people into ministry and create opportunities for people to be activated in ministry tools. God used her powerfully among us.

There were many valuable lessons learned during that season of formation. When I saw what Kristen had created in this curriculum, I could see how helpful this will be for others to experience this kind of life in the kingdom. The teachings are biblically sound and accompanied by activations. The activations will stretch you to encounter God through faith and, in my opinion, are a wonderful marriage of the practical and mystical.

When Kristen held her first *Kingdom Culture School of Ministry* class here at The House, it produced amazing results. There were miracles and lives transformed through the event. This was great, but what I appreciated most was the lasting fruit in lives after the event. Each one of the participants continued to use the ministry skills they learned. The testimonies kept rolling in well after the class ended!

At our church the curriculum has been utilized in a class format, small groups, as a seminar, and as an individual guide. We have used it in several nations around the world and it produces kingdom results every time! Each time God does wonders, heals people, and transforms lives.

The fact that you are reading this tells me that the Holy Spirit has been stirring your life to pursue something deeper. I believe this curriculum is going to be a wonderful addition to your journey. It takes courage to start anything new, but it's going to be worth it!

Till All Have Heard,

Pastor Jamey VanGelder
The House Church
iTheHouse.org

A Word from the Author

As a child, I collected music boxes and almost every single one of them played the same song, "It's a small world after all." It was my dream to grow up, leave my home state of Minnesota, and see people transformed in various nations of the world.

Now, many years later, I've traveled throughout Asia, Africa, Europe, and the Americas. I've seen:
- Buddhist girls in Japan accept Jesus when someone hugged them
- A California Starbucks customer healed while waiting for their coffee
- A Brazilian man's deaf ears open up and his heart receive Christ when someone simply told him that God loved him
- The salvation of an entire unreached Mozambican village after the local deaf and mute man heard and spoke
- My own life daily transformed by the goodness and kindness of God

I grew up Lutheran, got saved in and started attending a non-denominational church as a teenager, participated in an Assemblies of God youth group, studied the Bible with a fundamentalist church, and attended a Baptist university where I served with a student movement in Central America. I received my degree in socio-cultural and third world studies, and enjoyed spending time at Catholic monasteries.

I was first introduced to the supernatural through the International House of Prayer and Patricia King's Extreme Prophetic Glory School. I learned about healing by ministering with Randy Clark's Youth Power Invasion in Brazil, spent three years at the Bethel School of Supernatural Ministry (BSSM) in Redding, CA where I interned with Theresa Dedmon, and completed the Iris Harvest School of Missions with Heidi Baker in Mozambique. After all that I returned home to my beloved state of Minnesota and joined an amazing community called The House Church, under the leadership of Pastors Jamey & Nicole VanGelder.

After being a part of many different expressions of the body of Christ in many different nations, I've noticed a handful of key truths that, if present or absent, seem to make all the difference in the life of a believer. Simple truths like "God is good," "You are His good kid," "He still speaks and heals today," and "He has really good things to say to you," are eye-opening to many in the body of Christ.

I wanted to write a manual of some key principles that, if embraced, would bring the transformation of society through the lives of everyday believers. After over ten years of being involved with various ministry schools around the world, my aim was to create a "Swiss army knife" of a ministry school curriculum that could be used in individual or group settings, for ages ten and up, in any culture. My goal is for anyone to be able to pick up this book, look at a page, walk through it themselves, and easily lead others through the same experience without needing any preparation, props, or a long time to process the information.

Already, many who have gone through this material are walking in new levels of identity, sharing their faith and seeing others come to Christ more freely, experiencing physical healing, hearing from God for themselves, and seeing breakthroughs in their families. My heart is that these principles and activations will allow believers throughout many nations, church backgrounds, and cultures to embrace the culture of the kingdom and help align the tracks of their lives with the course of heaven.

With Joy on the Journey,
Kristen D'Arpa

Introduction

What is the kingdom of God? What is culture? How do I live out kingdom culture? What biblical principles is this book based on? How do I use this manual for myself or in a group? This introduction is an important foundation for the rest of the book. It shares key biblical principles that this course is built on and important guidelines for how to best use this manual for individuals or groups.

While this entire manual is designed for you to be able to jump right in, you are highly encouraged to take the time to read the introduction so that you can have the best experience possible with the rest of the book.

If you are facilitating this manual with a group of people, please take the time to go over this introduction for yourself ahead of time, and make sure to go over the Getting Started section on pages 11-12 together with your group. Please note that there is also a Facilitator's Guide and Additional Resources in the very back of the book.

The Kingdom of God

A kingdom can be defined as the dome (area, place, or territory of influence) in which a king reigns. Just as foreign ambassadors in another country are governed by the laws of their homeland, so we, as believers, are now part of a kingdom that has a different culture and standard of living than the world around us. The kingdom of God (also known as heaven or the kingdom of heaven) is a place of perfect love, joy, health, beauty, peace, creativity, and wholeness in every way. Our King and Father has called us to a life of royalty as His sons and daughters. As such, we must first change the way we think (our mindsets) and then the way we behave (our actions).

Small changes in our thinking are like train tracks switching from one track to another. When the tracks switch, the change is subtle. However, as the train continues on, the difference between one track or another can lead to the east or west coast of a nation. As we shift our mindsets according to the kingdom of God, the overflow of our lives will be the transformation of the world around us. Then we can fulfill the Lord's prayer that God's kingdom would come and His will would be done on earth as it is in heaven. We can experience heaven on earth in every area of our practical, everyday lives and also see that same transformation come to the people and places with whom we are in relationship.

The Kingdom of God in the Garden of Eden

The original way that we see the kingdom of God on earth is by looking at the **Garden of Eden** in Genesis 1-2. If we want to know God's heart for how He wants to relate to us and us to relate to others and the world, all we have to do is look at the Garden of Eden. Eden shows us God's original intent for people and the planet. Going back to the Garden of Eden can help us anchor our hearts and minds in a picture of what the kingdom can look like on earth. When we share with others about the kingdom of God, this can be a powerful place to start because the story of Eden in Genesis is simple, clear, and concrete enough that even a child can understand it. By looking at Eden we learn the following things about the kingdom of God.

God and People - God is the Creator and also our Father who brings children into the world (Gen. 1:27). He calls people "very good" and says that they are made in His image, and by this we know that both God and people are very good (Gen. 1:27). People are given responsibility and authority (to cultivate and keep the garden), are made to be in direct relationship with God, hear His voice clearly, and easily communicate with Him (Gen. 1:28; 2:19; 3:8-12). Before sin, there was no sickness or death. People knew their roles and responsibilities, understood their boundaries, and even created with God by naming the animals (Gen. 2:19). People were made male and female, both equally in His image, and got along with one another (Gen. 1:27). The word for "helper" when God made Eve (Gen. 2:18, 20) is the Hebrew word "ezer" (Strong's 5828) and is used fifteen times throughout Scripture to describe God helping Israel (this later points to how the Church is to relate to Jesus, not as a powerless slave, but as a powerful bride that brings great strength).

Creation - God spoke and life was created (Gen. 1:1). All of creation was good, produced fruit, and was at peace with itself. The garden needed to be tended but there was no strife. People were to lovingly care for creation and be in authority over all plants and animals.

The Enemy - The devil, first revealed as a snake, existed but did not have any power. All he could do was lie. He couldn't make anyone do anything but gained power over people when they believed and acted upon his lies, therefore giving him their authority (Gen. 1:28; 3:1-15; Matt. 4:8-9).

Everything was **good**! In the beginning, there was a good God with good people in a good world along with a bad, but powerless, enemy.

Choice and Free Will - There were two, specific trees in the Garden: the tree of the knowledge of good and evil, and the tree of life (Gen. 1:17; 3:22). The fruit of the tree of knowledge was not to be eaten. Even in a perfect world, God wanted man to choose His way, and God allowed man the power to make this choice rather than controlling him. Before eating of the forbidden tree, Adam and Eve received everything they needed out of **relationship** with God.

Sin - Adam and Eve chose to do what God told them not to do, and sought knowledge outside of a relationship with Him by eating of the tree of knowledge of good and evil (Gen. 3). When they did this they trusted the voice of the enemy more than the voice of their Father. Instead of ruling over the enemy they obeyed him and gave him their authority. They were filled with shame and hid from God. ***Sin isn't just about breaking God's rules, it is about breaking our relationship with Him and choosing to live in a way that causes us to walk away from Him.*** Whether in rebellion or religion, when we violate our relationship with God, we are wrong.

Consequences - God told Adam that in the day he ate of the tree of knowledge of good and evil, he would die. Romans 6:23a says, *"The wages of sin is death."* When we sin, there is always a consequence. This is not because God is angry and punishing us, but because it is actually what we deserve, just like when we are paid a wage for working a job. When they ate of the tree, Adam and Eve died spiritually and became ashamed of their nakedness. They had to leave the Garden of Eden, as God did not want them to eat from the tree of life and live forever in their fallen state (Gen. 3:23-24) and they also faced many other consequences laid out in Genesis 3. Even in the midst of their bad choices, God always stayed connected with Adam and Eve, communicating with them and their children, and was a part of their lives even after they left the Garden.

Restoration - God always makes a way for us to come back to Him. In Eden, He killed an animal to clothe Adam and Eve and cover their nakedness (Gen. 3:21). In killing an animal, you must spill its blood. This is a picture of all of the Old Testament sacrifices that only temporarily covered sin and is also a picture of what Jesus would someday do for us as our perfect sacrifice to take away all sin. He also promised that one day He would send a Savior to defeat the enemy (Gen. 3:15).

Jesus - Thousands of years later, Jesus came as a second Adam (1 Cor. 15:45-49), lived a perfect life, died on the cross, shed His blood to pay for the sins of the world, and fully defeated the devil when He rose from the dead (Col. 2:13-3:3). When we choose to surrender our lives to Jesus, we have access into the kingdom of God, back into Eden! We can now eat from the tree of life. Our spirits—and eventually, our redeemed bodies—will live forever (1 Cor. 15:51-54).

The Kingdom of God is like Eden. We may not live in an actual garden today, but Eden is a picture of the kingdom of God, which we can access in the Spirit. We are to cultivate, keep, and expand this kingdom garden into every area of our soul (mind, will, and emotions) and bodies, and then into the physical world around us. The Garden of Eden is where we (mankind) started, and it shows us God's original design. We live our lives in a world that does not look like this on the outside. As we first receive, then cultivate, then finally expand His kingdom garden in our hearts and minds, it will little by little impact the world around us, until the world looks more and more like heaven.

Are You Living in the Kingdom of God?

Have you fully received what Jesus has done for you? Have you asked God to forgive you not only for doing bad things, but also from walking away from Him and breaking your relationship? Have you fully surrendered your life to Jesus? Do you have God's garden of perfect peace, love, and joy living on the inside of you to the degree that you are able to demonstrate His kingdom to others? If not, or if you are not sure, or if you would like to recommit your life to Jesus after walking away from Him, pray this prayer out loud now:

> *"Thank you, Father God, that You are good and that You love me. I admit that I have done bad things, broken our relationship, and walked away from You. I believe, Jesus, that you paid for all of my sin on the cross and that You rose from the dead. I choose to come back into a relationship with You, turn away from the bad things I have done, surrender my life to You, and make You my one and only God. I receive Your forgiveness, forgive all those who have hurt me, and ask, Holy Spirit, that You fill me now. Amen."*

If you prayed this prayer for the first time, you are now a child of God and living in His kingdom! For anyone who prayed this prayer, please tell someone that you know well about your decision to surrender your life to Jesus. Pray and talk to God regularly, and listen for Him to speak to you. Get a Bible if you do not have one. Begin to read it regularly, starting in the book of Mark or John. Find a church that preaches about Jesus and get involved there. Regularly tell others about Jesus, and invite them to surrender their lives to Him as well.

Now that we have an understanding of the kingdom and are living in it, let's talk about culture.

Culture

Our culture is the lens (think of a person wearing a pair of glasses) **through which we see the world and the internal values that guide how and why we do everything that we do.** Culture is expressed through our actions, so much so that the best way to learn another culture is to immerse yourself not only in the heart of what that culture believes, but also in the activities of what that culture does. This is how the kingdom of God works. When we become believers, we enter into a new culture. When we enter this new culture, we are given a new way of seeing the world that shapes our values and our actions. This new kingdom culture has different beliefs and values, which are expressed in different ways of thinking and behaving than we have ever experienced before. It is now our responsibility, as believers in Jesus, to learn the mindsets and actions of this kingdom culture. This will take time for us to learn, but as we do the kingdom of heaven will be released through our lives!

Earthly Culture

I am a North American, white, non-denominational, female from the suburbs of Midwest America. My dad grew up around Cuban and Italian immigrants, and remembers the end of World War II. My grandfather was a first generation Italian-American. He was a lawyer, politician, and businessman who, later in life, planted churches and traveled the world speaking on behalf of the Full Gospel Business Men's Association. My grandmother was a tongue-talking, fiery, Bohemian-Norwegian. She was a beauty queen who prayed, prophesied, and handed out Gospel tracks to everyone she could find. My mom, on the other hand, came from a quiet, Scandinavian, Minnesota farming background, and grew up listening to stories from Lutheran missionaries who came through town. Her mother and her mother's mother prayed faithfully for all of the generations to come. Her father worked hard, tended the land as a farmer, lived a godly life, and gave his family a strong heritage of faith. Because of my cultural background, I have a passion for prayer, missions, travel, and eating tasty international food.

I am a combination of all the elements of my national, regional, family, ethnic, and religious backgrounds. This makes up my culture and how I see the world. Whether you are an African American male living in New York, a person of Japanese descent living in Brazil, or an indigenous tribal woman in the Philippines, you also have your own unique way of looking at the world. Even people who grow up in the same ethnic group and location may still come from different family cultures, depending on how their parents raised them and how their family members interacted with each other. Finally, in most societies there are also subcultures: groups within a society that participate in a certain lifestyle, have a defined social status, or define themselves around anything from sharing an interest in a common sport, type of music, or even membership in a gang.

Our culture tells us how to live our lives in everything we do like how far apart we stand when talking to another person, how involved our family is in our lives, what time we show up to events, and an infinite number of other areas.

Earthly Culture Meets Kingdom Culture

When we get saved and our earthly culture meets God's kingdom culture, there are a few important things for us to know. If we completely **accept** every part of our culture and add Christianity on top of it, that can be dangerous because many areas within our culture are not godly. If we completely **reject** our culture, or try to be like another culture, this is not good either because many parts of our culture are good. Paul said in Acts 15 that we don't need to become like another culture to walk with Jesus. The best thing we can do is to **transform** our culture. We can do that by being aware of the following areas.

Value What is Good
There are many beliefs and actions in our earthly culture that are in line with kingdom culture. It is okay if different cultures reflect God's kingdom in different ways. These things should be celebrated and honored!

Some Things Will Need to Change
Some of our cultural beliefs and actions are not in line with kingdom culture and will need to change. No matter how important or long standing these ways of thinking or behaving are, if they conflict with the kingdom of God, we must choose God's kingdom above our earthly culture.

The Lord will give each individual person wisdom on what needs to change, how that should look, and in what timing those changes should take place. You don't need to become like another earthly culture to please God, just like the Gentiles didn't need to be circumcised as Jews to become believers (Acts 15).

Some Areas are Neutral or Unclear
While many aspects of kingdom living are clearly defined, there are also many other areas that are not clearly defined. In these situations, we make decisions for what is okay to do or not okay to do out of our relationship with the Lord and out of honor for other people.

The Apostle Paul said that if it is important to one person to celebrate a certain holiday then they should celebrate it and do it as unto the Lord. However, if another person doesn't celebrate that holiday, then it is okay if it is just another day for them. Some people feel they must only eat certain kinds of food and other people eat every kind of food. Paul shows us that it is okay to live differently in our different cultures as long as we do not go against what the Bible clearly says, judge one another, or do something that causes another person to stumble.

> *One person esteems one day above another; another esteems every day alike. Let each be fully convinced in his own mind. He who observes the day, observes it to the Lord; and he who does not observe the day, to the Lord he does not observe it. He who eats, eats to the Lord, for he gives God thanks; and he who does not eat, to the Lord he does not eat, and gives God thanks. So then each of us shall give account of himself to God. Therefore let us not judge one another anymore, but rather resolve not to put a stumbling block or a cause to fall in our brother's way. - Romans 14:5-6, 12-13*

Learning Kingdom Culture

Just like babies learn how to crawl and then walk and run, as we are born into the kingdom of God it will be a process for us to learn, try, fail, succeed, and grow. Some examples that we can look at to give ourselves permission to be in a learning process (both in life in general and when using this manual) are how people learn to ride a bike or speak a new language. As we think about learning Kingdom Culture, here are a few verses that we can meditate on:

"For My thoughts are not your thoughts, Nor are your ways My ways," says the Lord. "For as the heavens are higher than the earth, so are My ways higher than your ways, and My thoughts than your thoughts." - Isaiah 55:8-9

But be doers of the word, and not hearers only, deceiving yourselves. For if anyone is a hearer of the word and not a doer, he is like a man observing his natural face in a mirror; for he observes himself, goes away, and immediately forgets what kind of man he was. - James 1:22-24

Learning to Ride a Bike

When learning to ride a bike, you only need a little bit of information and then a whole lot of practice. When I learned how to ride, I started with a small bike and training wheels. After a little while, my brother took off the training wheels and I had to learn how to ride in a different way. Eventually I got a bigger bike and my dad held onto it while I got on. He jogged alongside me, ready to catch me in case I fell. Soon, I no longer needed him to run alongside because I was able to ride all on my own.

Learning to live a kingdom lifestyle is like learning to ride a bike. You will need some instruction, a safe place to learn, and mostly, a whole lot of experience and practice.

Some people may be excited as they think about the new things they will experience and the freedom they will have to go to new places in the kingdom. Others may be a bit nervous, and hope that they won't fall down as they learn.

Throughout most of this manual you will be given just enough information for you to jump on and ride. Expect to learn new skills and travel at faster speeds than you ever have before. As with learning to ride a bike, give yourself permission to take some time to get used to new ways of thinking or behaving. It is okay if you try and fall; just get back up and try again!

For those of you who "already know how to ride a bike," know that there are always new gears you can try or different types of terrain to explore. If you are familiar or comfortable with a topic, then find a way to stretch or challenge yourself in that area by taking an activation to a further level, looking for new ways to apply it in your life, etc.

Learning a New Language

When learning a new language, you need to be able to both understand what someone else is saying and also speak back to them. What you know about the language is only as helpful as your ability to actually communicate in that language.

I spent a semester studying in Guatemala with a goal of learning Spanish. While studying language at a university level, I volunteered at a daycare and practiced speaking with four and five-year-olds. By the end of the semester, I had enough credits for a Spanish minor but only the ability to have a conversation on a pre-school level. Like learning to ride a bike, what I really needed wasn't more information, but simply more application and practice.

When I had fun, had a good sense of humor with myself, and applied what I learned as I learned it, the learning process was enjoyable. Whether I fully mastered what I was learning or not, I was engaged in the process and continued growing. One time, I went around the market asking how much certain items cost. I only discovered later that I was actually asking, "How much do I cost?" Yikes!!! While I felt a little embarrassed, I was proud of myself that I tried a new skill and took a big enough risk to fail at it.

There were other times when I tried to be perfect in my language learning, and this made my process difficult and frustrating. At one point, the person taking my order in a fast food restaurant couldn't understand what I was ordering. Instead of being patient with myself and continuing to try, I got upset, left the building, and didn't eat lunch. This idea that I needed to be perfect in order to speak was foolish. Even as a fluent English speaker, there are still words and rules of my language that I continue to learn.

Learning to live a kingdom lifestyle is like learning a new language. We need to study, but to truly learn we must practice both listening and speaking that language as much as we can. If I know hundreds of vocabulary words but cannot talk to even a child, all of my learning has not actually helped me. However, if I can start with understanding and speaking even the most basic of phrases, I can begin to interact within the new culture!

As it is in learning a new language, you may need to start by simply becoming familiar with basic kingdom concepts (i.e. understanding the language when you hear others speak it). If you are already familiar with and able to understand these concepts, then practice doing (i.e. speaking) them in a new way. If you are comfortable both in "understanding" and in "speaking," then learn each concept well enough that you could teach it to someone else and help them activate it in their lives.

Biblical Overview

God's Word is alive and powerful! The Bible shows us what God's kingdom is like and how we are to live. If we truly believe the Bible, we will speak, do, teach, and demonstrate what the Word of God says. The goal of this manual is to root and ground you in both the Word of God and in the practical demonstration of it in your personal life. The topical overview of biblical principles in this manual is powerful, both for new believers who are looking to grow in new truths, as well as mature believers who are looking to go deeper and teach others. Here are some of the ways in which we will interact with the Bible in this material, and some foundational truths we will build upon.

How the Bible Quotes the Bible

The Bible, even when it quotes itself, often uses principles from one situation to explain something specific going on in a very different situation. For example, in Acts 2 the Apostle Peter quotes Joel 2 to explain Pentecost:

> *And they were all filled with the Holy Spirit and began to speak with other tongues, as the Spirit gave them utterance. And when this sound occurred, the multitude came together, and*

were confused, because everyone heard them speak in his own language. But Peter, standing up with the eleven, raised his voice and said to them, "Men of Judea and all who dwell in Jerusalem, let this be known to you, and heed my words. For these are not drunk, as you suppose, since it is only the third hour of the day.

But this is what was spoken by the prophet Joel: 'And it shall come to pass in the last days, says God, that I will pour out of My Spirit on all flesh; your sons and your daughters shall prophesy, your young men shall see visions, your old men shall dream dreams. And on My menservants and on My maidservants I will pour out My Spirit in those days; and they shall prophesy. I will show wonders in heaven above and signs in the earth beneath: Blood and fire and vapor of smoke.'" - Acts 2:4, 6, 14-19

In this passage, no one is dreaming dreams, having visions, prophesying, or doing any of the things listed, however it is used to explain everyone speaking in tongues and seeming to be drunk. In 1 Corinthians 9:9, Paul quotes Deuteronomy 25:4, "You shall not muzzle an ox while it treads out the grain." He uses it to prove a principle for taking care of people.

Throughout this course we will look at many passages of Scripture. From the principles of those verses, we will draw out applications for our lives today. Some applications may directly apply to the passages and some, like the examples above, may apply indirectly.

Biblical Principles This Course is Based On

The Bible is the Word of God
All Scripture is given by inspiration of God, and is profitable for doctrine, for reproof, for correction, for instruction in righteousness. - 2 Timothy 3:16

God's Word is Alive and Powerful
For the Word of God is living and powerful, and sharper than any two-edged sword, piercing even to the division of soul and spirit, and of joints and marrow, and is a discerner of the thoughts and intents of the heart. - Hebrews 4:12

Renewing Our Minds Brings Transformation
And do not be conformed to this world, but be transformed by the renewing of your mind, that you may prove what is that good and acceptable and perfect will of God. - Romans 12:2

What We Believe We Speak
And since we have the same spirit of faith, according to what is written, "I believed and therefore I spoke," we also believe and therefore speak. - 2 Corinthians 4:13

For with the heart one believes unto righteousness, and with the mouth confession is made unto salvation. - Romans 10:10

For out of the abundance of the heart the mouth speaks. - Matthew 12:34b

What we believe is true we will say out loud. It is important to say what we know to be true even if we do not feel like it is true yet. By speaking, we strengthen what we believe and think. When we change our thoughts, our emotions will eventually change as well. Throughout this course we will make declarations and speak out loud the truths that we are learning to God, ourselves, and others.

What We Believe We Do
What does it profit, my brethren, if someone says he has faith but does not have works? Can faith save him? If a brother or sister is naked and destitute of daily food, and one of you says to them, "Depart in peace, be warmed and filled," but you do not give them the things which are needed for the body, what does it profit? Thus also faith by itself, if it does not have works, is dead. - James 2:14-17

Most assuredly, I say to you, he who believes in Me, the works that I do he will do also; and greater works than these he will do, because I go to My Father. - John 14:12

If we really believe something is true, we will take action on that belief, just like if I believe a chair is real, I will take action by putting all of my weight to sit on that chair. Throughout this course, we will constantly be doing and activating kingdom principles, and demonstrating them in a variety of specific and concrete ways.

We Walk in Power and Love With God and People
For the kingdom of God is not in word but in power. - 1 Corinthians 4:20

For God has not given us a spirit of fear, but of power and of love and of a sound mind. - 2 Timothy 1:7

And though I have the gift of prophecy, and understand all mysteries and all knowledge, and though I have all faith, so that I could remove mountains, but have not love, I am nothing. - 1 Corinthians 13:2

And we have known and believed the love that God has for us. God is love, and he who abides in love abides in God, and God in him. . . We love Him because He first loved us. If someone says, "I love God," and hates his brother, he is a liar; for he who does not love his brother whom he has seen, how can he love God whom he has not seen. And this commandment we have from Him: that he who loves God must love his brother also. - 1 John 4:16,19-21

The kingdom of God is demonstrated in power and expressed through love. As we receive the love that God has for us, we are able to give that love away to those around us. People are important, and no matter how powerful we or our gifts are, these gifts must always be used out of a place of love, and aimed at loving God and others.

We Walk in Relationship with the Author
Now it happened on the second Sabbath after the first that He went through the grain-fields. And His disciples plucked the heads of grain and ate them, rubbing them in their hands. And some of the Pharisees said to them, "Why are you doing what is not lawful to do on the Sabbath?" But Jesus answering them said, "Have you not even read this, what David did when he was hungry, he and those who were with him: how he went into the house of God, took and ate the showbread, and also gave some to those with him, which is not lawful for any but the priests to eat?" And He said to them, "The Son of Man is also Lord of the Sabbath." - Luke 6:1-5

The Pharisees knew God's law (or their interpretation of it), but did not have a relationship with Him. They did not know who Jesus was when He came in the flesh. They elevated rules and religion above the law of love, often accusing the Word made flesh (Jesus) of breaking the very law He embodied.

The Lord is a person, and while His Word is the foundation for everything, He is also bigger than His Book. Everything in our lives should line up with the principles of Scripture, but not everything in our lives will be directly found in the Bible. (John 21:25 says we don't even have written accounts of all that Jesus did.) Just like in Acts 2, many principles in Scripture may teach us a truth, but that truth will look different as it is expressed in different people's lives. Jesus is the Word made flesh; He is a living person. We have a relationship with Him and follow Him as He walks with each of us in our daily lives.

Kingdom Alignment

In the kingdom of heaven there is an established order to how things are done. When we operate within this order, there is a greater alignment, ease of ministry, and fruitfulness from heaven to earth. **As believers, we want to operate from the kingdom of heaven** (the realm of the Holy Spirit and our redeemed spirit), and **not primarily from** the spiritual realm of the angelic/demonic (which is also the realm of your soul) or from our physical world and bodies (which, like your soul, should receive care but not run your life).

The Kingdom of Heaven

The kingdom of heaven is the highest heaven (sometimes called the third heaven from 2 Corinthians 12:2). It is where the throne room is, the place from where God rules and reigns and where believers are seated in Christ. It is the eternal and timeless realm and a place of perfection, peace, order, and love. **This is the realm from where we declare, pray, prophesy, heal, and testify.**

*. . . and what is the exceeding greatness of His power toward us who believe, according to the working of His mighty power which He worked in Christ when He raised Him from the dead and **seated Him at His right hand in the heavenly places.** - Ephesians 1:19-20*

My Spirit

My spirit is my true and eternal self. As a believer my spirit is sealed by the Holy Spirit (Ephesians 4:30), made new the moment I received Christ, and now lives inside of Jesus as He is seated in heavenly places. My spirit is like the "Holy of Holies" in the Old Testament temple.

For what man knows the things of a man except the spirit of the man which is in him? Even so no one knows the things of God except the Spirit of God. - 1 Corinthians 2:11

And you He made alive, who were dead in trespasses and sins . . . and raised us up together, and made us sit together in the heavenly places in Christ Jesus. - Ephesians 2:1, 6

The Spiritual Realm

The spiritual realm is the realm of the demonic as well as angelic and the place of spiritual warfare (sometimes called the second heaven). It is the highest level of spiritual truth for other religions. Things that happen in this realm are real but not the highest level of truth. We can be aware of what is happening there, but it is not where we ultimately focus. We focus on Jesus and His kingdom more than what is going on with angels and demons.

*. . . which He worked in Christ when He raised Him from the dead and seated Him at His right hand in the heavenly places, **far above all principality and power and might and dominion, and every name that is named** . . . - Ephesians 1:20-21a*

And He said to them, "I saw Satan fall like lightning from heaven. Behold, I give you the authority to trample on serpents and scorpions, and over all the power of the enemy, and nothing shall by any means hurt you. . ." - Luke 10:18-19

My Soul

My soul is comprised of my mind, will, and emotions which are in the process of being renewed day by day. My soul is like the Promised Land given to Israel; while it was fully theirs they still had to kick out giants, possess the land, and maintain it. If we believe the lies of the enemy and allow him to "stay in our land" we can choose to allow him access to our lives (Luke 11:24-26; Ephesians 4:27; Romans 12:1-2).

Jesus said to him, "You shall love the Lord your God with all your heart, with all your soul, and with all your mind." - Matthew 22:37

Now may the God of peace Himself sanctify you completely; and may your whole spirit, soul, and body be preserved blameless at the coming of our Lord Jesus Christ. - 1 Thessalonians 5:23

The Earth/Physical Realm

The physical earth or the natural world (sometimes called the first heaven), is what we can see and judge from our five senses. God created the world and put us in charge of stewarding and caring for the earth.

In the beginning God created the heavens and the earth. . . . Then God blessed them, and God said to them, "Be fruitful and multiply; fill the earth and subdue it; have dominion over the fish of the sea, over the birds of the air, and over every living thing that moves on the earth." - Genesis 1:1, 28

My Body

My body is my physical self and natural senses. It is like the "temple" in the Old Testament and should be cared for as such.

Or do you not know that your body is the temple of the Holy Spirit who is in you, whom you have from God, and you are not your own? For you were bought at a price; therefore glorify God in your body and in your spirit, which are God's. - 1 Corinthians 6:19-20

About This Manual

Topics and Concepts
This manual is broken down into various topical sections, and then specific kingdom concepts or lessons within each section. Starting with Identity, the manual builds topic by topic, and ends with Societal Transformation. Some sections will be very brief and give high level overviews. Other sections will go into many different, more in-depth concepts for how these topics could be activated. There is a detailed Facilitator's Guide as well as an Additional Information section in the back of the book.

Format
Each concept is covered in a one page lesson with Scripture, a brief Description, Activation(s) (i.e. a way to experientially "do" that concept), and an Application. Some lessons offer resources for further study, a designated space for notes or journaling, or an additional resource page. Concepts are laid out systematically but can be done in any order.

How to Use this Manual
If you are participating in a live-taught Kingdom Culture School, you will be using this manual together with a group of believers. While we will do our best to review each section, there may be areas left for you to review on your own, at a later time. These lessons can also be completed as a daily devotional (although you will need to engage with others for many of the activations), in a small group setting, or as supplemental lessons for youth groups, Bible studies, children's programs, or ministry schools. This can be used for ages ten and up, in any culture, or modified for younger children. For information on bringing a live-taught school or event to your area, planting a school, licenses to reproduce any part of this material, or to help with language translations please contact us at KristenDArpa.com.

This material is designed to be like a "Swiss army knife" or "Legos" in that you can customize it to your specific setting in whatever way is the most helpful for you. The goal is that anyone could pick up this book, look at a page, walk through it themselves, and easily lead others through the same experience without needing preparation, props, or a long time to process the information. When facilitating this material in groups, we typically cover three to four concepts per hour. This allows fifteen to twenty minutes per topic, including about eight to ten minutes for activation. The idea is to have _brief_ instruction times so there's just enough understanding to activate the group members, keep things moving, and not spend a long time teaching. While activating, it is important to apply each concept as personally, specifically, and concretely as possible. When doing drawing activations, know that it is not about skill, so simple drawings work great. In keeping with these values, you are free to adjust how you use this material to suit the needs of your particular group. Please see the Facilitator's Guide in the back of the book for more information on how to use this manual with groups.

Getting Started
The following are important guidelines and ground rules for everyone who will use this material. If using this in a group, please take the time to read through this section together with the participants.

Only Good
When completing each activation, participants agree to only speak, pray, prophesy, or declare good things. Philippians 4:8-9 tells us to only think about those things that are good and right. In 1 Corinthians 14:3, we see that prophecy is meant to bring encouragement and comfort. If you receive or sense something that is negative in any way (something bad happening, something someone is doing wrong, etc.), DO NOT pray, declare, or prophesy it AT ALL. We rest in knowing that light dispels all darkness, so we have no need to focus on or even mention the darkness. We also do not give any words of direction or correction to others. If a person needs to be confronted or an issue needs to be addressed and you are in a trusted relationship with that person, you can talk to them privately, as a friend, on your own time. However, within this course, negative information should NEVER be shared through a prayer or prophetic word.

Embrace the New and Review
- **Risk**: If something is new or stretching for you, take a deep breath and give it a try! Like Peter walking on the water towards Jesus, you will be taking bold steps. We will celebrate that you took a risk to try something new, regardless of whether or not you are successful.
- **Go deeper**: If you already know **about** a topic, check to see if you are actively **living** it out in this current moment. Be open to learning and applying even more of that concept in your life.
- **Deeper still:** If you already understand something and are applying it to your life, then **stretch** yourself a bit further in that concept and/or learn it well enough that you could **teach** it to others.

Group Participation Guidelines
- **Partners:** Do each activation with one other person. Plan to share for about two to three minutes each. Be brief so both of you have time to share. Change partners with every new principle.
- **Confidentiality:** What others share with us about themselves will stay with us. We will not share it with others unless we have asked for and received the other person's permission.
- **Safety:** This is a safe place to try, fail, and succeed wildly!
- **Powerful:** You are powerful and have the right to judge what others share with you. You are the one who decides if, or how, you will receive those things.
- **Feedback:** You can give loving feedback to others. E.g. "That was so encouraging!" Or, "That would have felt more encouraging if you worded it this way or took out this part." Or, "I'm not sure if that applies to me or not, but I will pray about it."

Beginning Declaration
Genesis 1:3 tells us that God spoke and worlds (light, plants, people, etc.) were created. Proverbs 18:21 tells us that life and death are in the power of the tongue. Declarations are kingdom truths we say out loud over ourselves or another person, a place, or a situation. Just like God spoke creation into existence, speaking God's words aloud actually creates that reality in the midst of our situation.

Declare the following over yourself out loud:

> "Lord I invite you into every area of my life. I declare that all of my ways of thinking, feeling, and behaving are being transformed to look like Your kingdom."

> "I choose to honor and celebrate my national, ethnic, church, and family cultures. Whatever areas of those cultures line up with the culture of Your kingdom, I choose to keep. Whatever areas do not line up with Your kingdom, I choose to lay down, and I ask You to replace those with truth."

> "I give myself permission to not have to look, think, or act like anyone else. I agree that how You made me is good and that You speak to me and work through me in ways that are beautiful, powerful, and unique. I declare that I am safe to step out into new areas of risk and freedom in learning to walk out the kingdom of God."

> "I bless my spirit and call it to attention to live from the reality of heaven and rule over my soul and body. I bless my mind to easily think new thoughts and understand new truths. I declare that I have the mind of Christ. I bless my will to be quick to do what God says. I bless my emotions to be in line with the heart of the Father. I bless my body to be awake, alert, and healthy. I declare new pathways in my brain to be created."

Let's Jump in!
Here are a few final ground rules to remember:
- **Patient**: Be patient and kind with yourself and others in this learning process.
- **Risk**: Celebrate risk versus success.
- **Fun**: Have fun! Have a good sense of humor and enjoy trying new things!

Identity

*Therefore, if anyone is in Christ, he is a new creation; old things have
passed away; behold, all things have become new.*
- 2 Corinthians 5:17

*Behold what manner of love the Father has bestowed on us,
that we should be called children of God!*
- 1 John 3:1a

Everything in the kingdom starts with knowing first who God is, and then who we are. As we come to know the Father, Son, and Holy Spirit as a good God who has good things for us, we can rest in the love that God has for us as His dear children. Just as Jesus the Son of God reflects who the Father truly is, so we, as sons of God, get to show the world who the Father is through our day-to-day lives. We can only give away what we have first received, so before we do anything, we need to understand who God made us to be.

When we know who we are, we can live at peace with God, ourselves, and others, and therefore more powerfully impact the world around us. We can be our authentic selves without the pressure to perform for God or people, and live free of comparing ourselves to others in order to feel good about who we are. Knowing our identity means knowing that we are the Father's well-loved son or daughter, that we have all of His approval and goodness behind us, and that we can boldly and courageously be who our Father has made us to be! When we are secure in our identity, it is easier to think about ourselves less and lay down our lives for those around us.

In this section, we will look briefly at who God is, what He does, and who we are in Him.

Resources
Become You and any messages by Pastor Nathanael White (Personal Identity). NathanaelWhite.com
Go Fam Ministries (Personal, Family, and Marriage Identity). GoFam.org
The Supernatural Ways of Royalty by Kris Vallotton.

God is Good

Scripture
So God created man in His own image; in the image of God He created him; male and female He created them...God saw all that He had made, and it was very good. And there was evening, and there was morning - the sixth day. - Genesis 1:27, 31

Oh, taste and see that the Lord is good; Blessed is the man who trusts in Him! - Psalm 34:8

The Lord is good, a stronghold in the day of trouble; and He knows those who trust in Him. - Nahum 1:7

Description
God has always been God and, as such, He has always been good. God is both a Creator and a good, good Father. God isn't angry, frustrated, or displeased with you. God is in a good mood. He loves you, is happy with you, and wants good things for you! You are His precious son or daughter, and He loves you so very much!

Activation 1
- How do you see God?
- Do you see Him as good, happy, and well pleased with you? If not, take a moment to ask the Lord to forgive you for not seeing Him as good.
- Ask Him to reveal Himself to you as a good and happy God.
- Picture yourself before the Lord. Imagine Him smiling at you and being well pleased with you!

Activation 2
- Draw a picture about what God looks like to you as a good God. You can draw one picture or draw separate pictures about what the Father, Son, and Holy Spirit each look like to you, as a good God.
- Share with a partner what you drew.

Application
The first lie the devil told Eve in Eden was that God was not good. This lie is often still the root of many things that lead us away from God. If we truly know that God is good at all times and in every area of our lives, we will have a hope-filled foundation to build our lives on. If you find yourself struggling with an area of your life, ask yourself if you are truly believing that God is good, even in the midst of that struggle.

God Only Does Good Things

Scripture
God saw all that He had made, and it was very good. - Genesis 1:31a

If you then, being evil, know how to give good gifts to your children, how much more will your Father who is in heaven give good things to those who ask Him! - Matthew 7:11

Every good gift and every perfect gift is from above, and comes down from the Father of lights, with whom there is no variation or shadow of turning. Let no one say when he is tempted, "I am tempted by God"; for God cannot be tempted by evil, nor does He Himself tempt anyone. - James 1:17, 13

And we know that all things work together for good to those who love God. - Romans 8:28a

Description
If God is a good God, then it is also true that He only does, says, and gives good things. That means if something is bad or evil, it can't possibly have come from God. God can't give someone cancer or sickness, because He doesn't possess it. Likewise, God does not give people guilt, shame, poverty, sadness, or any other bad thing to try to teach them a lesson. God works everything together for good, but He does not cause everything that happens. Bad things come from the devil (who is NOT an equal with God) and are the result of our fallen world, or are consequences from bad choices that we or others have made.

Activation 1
- Make a list of ten good things in your life and spend time thanking God for them.
- Write down any bad or negative things that you've thought were from God.
- One at a time, cross them out.
- As you do so, ask God to forgive you for believing He caused those things.
- Ask Him to help you see how He is working these things together for your good.

Activation 2
- Read Philippians 4:8 from The Passion Translation below out loud.
  - *So keep your thoughts continually fixed on all that is authentic and real, honorable and admirable, beautiful and respectful, pure and holy, merciful and kind. And fasten your thoughts on every glorious work of God, praising him always.*
- Now, read it as a declaration about yourself saying, "I keep my thoughts . . ."
- Pray the verse back to God, out loud. Ask Him to help you see the good He is doing in your life.

Application
Because God is good and only does good, it is important for us to make sure we are thinking good and healthy thoughts, moment by moment. As you go throughout your day, use Philippians 4:8 as a guideline for the kinds of things you let yourself think about.

Made in God's Image

Scripture
So God created man in His own image; in the image of God He created him; male and female He created them. - Genesis 1:27

For the Lord is good; His mercy is everlasting, and His truth endures to all generations. - Psalm 100:5

Description
Since we are made in God's image, every good thing we know about God's nature also applies to our true selves. For example, God is the Creator, so that makes us creative. God is the Healer, so that makes us healers. We are not God—nor are we all-knowing and all-powerful—but we are like Him. Genesis also tells us that men and women are equally made in God's image.

Activation 1
- What are some of the things that you know to be true about God?
    - On a piece of paper write, "God is" at the top right and make a list about Him, beneath.
- Since you are made in God's image, most of those same things are also true about you!
    - To the left of each area you wrote about God, write, "I am," to signify that those things are also true about who you are. Here is an example:

I	am (as)	God is:
I	am	Kind
I	am	Happy
I	am	Smart

- If any of the areas you wrote about God aren't exactly true about you, you can write a note next to them or adjust them. E.g. God is all powerful and I am not, but because I am made in His image, I am powerful. God is love and I am loving.
- Ask God, "Lord, please show me every day how I am like You."
- Read your list out loud over yourself. Share what you wrote with a partner.

Activation 2
- Put on some soaking music (i.e. peaceful background music).
- Ask the Lord, "What were You thinking when You created me?"
- Ask Him why He made you and what good plans He has for your life.
- Write down what He shows you and share it with a partner.

Application
Jesus later came and was not only made in the image of God, but also lived a perfect life as God on the earth. In doing this, He restored us back to our inheritance as God's kids. Jesus showed us what a normal life as one of God's kids can look like. We need to see every part of ourselves as made in God's image. When we see this as true in our hearts, receiving what Jesus did for us, we won't have to fight our behavior, but will live our lives like Jesus lived His life.

Loved, and Loving

Scripture
God is love, and he who abides in love abides in God, and God in him. - 1 John 4:16b

Love is large and incredibly patient. Love is gentle and consistently kind to all. It refuses to be jealous when blessing comes to someone else. Love does not brag about one's achievements nor inflate its own importance. Love does not traffic in shame and disrespect, nor selfishly seek its own honor. Love is not easily irritated or quick to take offense. Love joyfully celebrates honesty and finds no delight in what is wrong. Love is a safe place of shelter, for it never stops believing the best for others. Love never takes failure as defeat, for it never gives up. Love never fails. - 1 Corinthians 13:4-8a TPT

Description
God is love. Everything God does is loving, because that is who He is. We are His dearly loved children, and are made in His image. We must first know God as a God of love. Then we receive the love that He has for us as a free gift, not because of anything that we do to earn it. Finally, out of this overflow we can give our lives away as lovers of God, ourselves, and others.

Activation 1
- Read 1 Corinthians 13 above out loud but say, "God," "Jesus," or "Father God" in place of "love" and make each phrase specific to you. E.g. "<u>God (or Jesus or Father God)</u> is gentle and consistently kind to <u>me</u>." As you say each line, ask Him to show you what it looks like for Him to relate to you in this way. Close your eyes and picture it.
- Say to the Lord out loud, "Lord, please help me receive the love that You have for me."
- Take a deep breath and be still. Close your eyes and rest in His love for you.
- Do the above again and make each line specific by adding in more details about your life. E.g. "Jesus is incredibly patient with me even when I get angry and feel behind at work."

Activation 2
- Use each line of the Corinthians passage above to talk to the Lord, out loud, about how much you love Him. For example, "God (or Father or Jesus), I love that You are so large that nothing scares You. Jesus, I love that You are patient because it is who You are. Father, I love Your gentleness." Go into as much detail as you can about your love for Him.

Activation 3
- You are made in God's image, so read the above passage again out loud, and this time say "I am" in each of those places. E.g. "I am gentle and consistently kind to all."

Activation 4
- Ask the Lord to bring to mind specific people that He is calling you to love and how He wants you to practically demonstrate 1 Corinthians 13 to them. Share this with a partner.

Application
When we receive God's love we can love Him back and more easily "love the one" who is in front of us. Love looks like something and should be tangible when we receive and give it away.

*Message inspired by Heidi Baker, Iris Global, IrisGlobal.org

Connecting with the Lord

Scripture
Then Jesus answered and said to them, "Most assuredly, I say to you, the Son can do nothing of Himself, but what He sees the Father do; for whatever He does, the Son also does in like manner. . . all things that I heard from My Father I have made known to you. . . My sheep hear My voice, and I know them, and they follow Me." - John 5:19; 15:15b; 10:27

Description
Jesus always knew what His Father wanted to share with Him. As sons and daughters of God we, too, can listen and look to see what our Father wants to communicate with us as well as hear from Jesus as His sheep. Whatever we sense God is telling us should always line up with the Bible (2 Timothy 3:16-17), be rooted in love (1 Corinthians 13), and be confirmed by other spiritually mature believers (2 Corinthians 13:1). As we stay in connection to the Lord, the Bible, and other believers, we will grow in learning how to hear, understand, and apply what God tells us. As we hear from God for ourselves it is important to invite two or three trusted friends or spiritual advisors into our process. We should regularly share with them what we feel like God is speaking to us and they can help confirm if it is from the Lord or not.

Activation 1
- Get something you can write with and do these four steps:
  1. **Be still and quiet yourself before the Lord.**
  2. **Picture yourself with Jesus and look to see what He does or shows you.**
     Position your heart to both receive His love and love Him back. You can imagine you are with Him in a Bible story that you know, picture Him sitting next to you, or ask Him to show you a place in your mind where He wants to meet with you.
  3. **Ask Him a specific question and write it down.**
     Examples: "Jesus, what do You want to speak to me?" "What do you want to show me today?" "What do You love about me?"
  4. **Write down all the spontaneous thoughts, senses, and pictures that come to mind.**
     - Do not filter or question what you get, just write it all down. Continue to picture Jesus and stay connected to Him. You can write more questions and more answers.
- Read what you have written and ask the Lord what parts were Him speaking to you and if there were any parts that were not Him speaking. Share your writing with a partner.

Activation 2
- Ask the Lord to show you two or three mature Christians you know who you could ask to regularly read what you feel God is telling you, to both confirm and lovingly question it.
- At first, send them everything you write once a week. Later on, only send them areas you need discernment on. Always send them everything you've written without editing it.

Application
As you begin, keep your questions general like the ones above. As you grow in your ability to hear you can ask the Lord more specific things like, "What job should I apply for?" Ask Him questions about yourself and your choices and not about what others will do.

Resource
* Lesson taken from the book, *Four Keys to Hearing God's Voice* by Mark and Patti Virkler

My Old Self is Gone, and I am New

Scripture
Therefore, if anyone is in Christ, he is a new creation; old things have passed away; behold, all things have become new. - 2 Corinthians 5:17

I have been crucified with Christ; it is no longer I who live, but Christ lives in me; and the life which I now live in the flesh I live by faith in the Son of God, who loved me and gave Himself for me. - Galatians 2:20

Knowing this, that our old man was crucified with Him, that the body of sin might be done away with, that we should no longer be slaves of sin. - Romans 6:6

Description
When I surrendered my life to Jesus, it was as if I was literally with Him on the cross. There He paid for all of my sin and my entire old nature of pain, distance from God, and wanting to do bad things. After His crucifixion, the disciples went to His tomb to find His body, but they could not find Him because He had risen from the dead. When He later appeared to them, He had a new, redeemed body. As a believer, this is now true of me spiritually. Just like Jesus received a new redeemed body after His resurrection, I now have a new, redeemed nature. The person I used to be died with Jesus and was buried. I cannot even find that person anymore, because the tomb is empty! I am now resurrected with Jesus into a new way of living and being. I have His redeemed nature and am a new creation.

Activation 1
Meditate on this passage: *"My old identity has been co-crucified with Messiah and no longer lives; for the nails of his cross crucified me with him. And now the essence of this new life is no longer mine, for the Anointed One lives his life through me—we live in union as one! My new life is empowered by the faith of the Son of God who loves me so much that he gave himself for me, and dispenses his life into mine!"* - Galatians 2:20 TPT

Activation 2
- Get out a piece of paper and divide it into thirds.
- In the left section draw a cross. Now draw BOTH Jesus and you on the cross together.
- By the cross write the things that were true of your old self, going into detail if you can.
- In the middle section draw a tomb with the bodies of you and Jesus inside and a stone in front. Look at the picture and take a moment to grieve the loss of your old self. That person will never exist in the same way again and you will never live like they lived. Ask the Lord, "Jesus, what do You want to show me here?" Journal what He shows you.
- In the right section draw an empty tomb with the stone rolled away. Draw you and Jesus walking away from the tomb together. Ask Jesus, "Show me how You see my new self." Journal what He shares with you. Write down, in detail, what your new creation self is like.
- Share with a partner.

Application
When you are tempted to think that you are the same person you used to be, or that you struggle with the same problems as your old self, remember that the tomb is empty. See yourself resurrected with Jesus as a new person.

Adopted Into the Family

Scripture
For you did not receive the spirit of bondage again to fear, but you received the Spirit of adoption by whom we cry out, "Abba, Father." - Romans 8:15

I will not leave you orphans; I will come to you. - John 14:18

. . .that we might receive the adoption as sons. And because you are sons, God has sent forth the Spirit of His Son into your hearts, crying out, "Abba, Father!" Therefore you are no longer a slave but a son, and if a son, then an heir of God through Christ. - Galatians 4:5b-7

Description
Before we knew the Lord, we were spiritually orphans. As believers, we are adopted as sons into God's family! In the kingdom, both males and females are "sons" of God just like all believers are the bride of Christ. In Roman society (where the Apostle Paul was a citizen) once a son was adopted, he could never be un-adopted. He was given the same full inheritance as the natural-born children, his past was completely erased, an all of his debts were paid. An orphan spirit is at the root of most of our personal, relational, and societal issues. A person with an orphan spirit looks to other people (like a leader, spouse, child, friend, or even the church or government) to meet their needs. A person living as a son of God knows they are loved, chosen, and accepted by the Father and can love God and others out of that overflow. Sons know they have full access to everything in the Father's house and that they receive the same love, affection, and inheritance as Jesus.

Activation 1
- Draw an adoption certificate and put your name on it.
- Speak these truths over yourself. You can add in any other words that come to mind.
  "I am no longer (orphan spirit) _____.   I am   (spirit of adoption) _____."

Unloved and Unwanted	Loved and Wanted
Insecure and Rejected	Secure and Accepted
Jealous of others	One who celebrates with others
Working for approval	One who works from approval
An orphan	A beloved son/daughter!

- Hear the Father say to you, "This is my beloved son /daughter, in whom I am well pleased."
- Close your eyes and rest in knowing that the Father loves you and you are His precious child.

Activation 2
- Look at the sheet next to this page and circle all of the places that you relate to.
- Read the places on the center and right hand column over yourself, declaring the truth out loud. E.g. "The image of God I see is of a loving Father."

Application
An orphan spirit cannot be cast out. Rather, it can only be loved out, because only perfect love removes all fear. Spend time meditating on who God says you are and how much He loves you. You may need to spend some time forgiving your earthly father for ways he did not model the heavenly Father to you. Allow the heavenly Father to heal you and love you.

Resources
Healing the Orphan Spirit by Leif Hetland and *Experiencing the Father's Embrace* by Jack Frost

The Heart of an Orphan   The Heart of Sonship

The Heart of an Orphan		The Heart of Sonship
See God as Master	IMAGE OF GOD	See God as a loving Father
Independent / Self-reliant	DEPENDENCY	Interdependent / Acknowledges Need
Live by the Love of Law	THEOLOGY	Live by the Law of Love
Insecure / Lack peace	SECURITY	Rest and Peace
Strive for the praise, approval, and acceptance of man	NEED FOR APPROVAL	Totally accepted in God's love and justified by grace
A need for personal achievement as you seek to impress God and others, or no motivation to serve at all	MOTIVE FOR SERVICE	Service that is motivated by a deep gratitude for being unconditionally loved and accepted by God
Duty and earning God's favor or no motivation at all	MOTIVE BEHIND CHRISTIAN DISCIPLINES	Pleasure and delight
Must be holy to have God's favor, thus increasing a sense of shame and guilt	MOTIVE FOR PURITY	Want to be holy; do not want anything to hinder intimate relationship with God
Self-rejection from comparing yourself to others	SELF-IMAGE	Positive and affirmed because you know you have such value to God
Seek comfort in counterfeit affections: addictions, compulsions, escapism, busyness, hyper-religious activity	SOURCE OF COMFORT	Seek times of quietness and solitude to rest in the Father's presence and love
Competition, rivalry, and jealousy toward others' success and position	PEER RELATIONSHIPS	Humility and unity as you value others and are able to rejoice in their blessings and success
Accusation and exposure in order to make yourself look good by making others look bad	HANDLING OTHERS' FAULTS	Love covers as you seek to restore others in a spirit of love and gentleness
See authority as a source of pain; distrustful toward them and lack a heart attitude of submission	VIEW OF AUTHORITY	Respectful and honoring; you see them as ministers of God for good in your life
Difficulty receiving admonition; you must be right so you easily get your feelings hurt and close your spirit to discipline	VIEW OF ADMONITION	See the receiving of admonition as a blessing and need in your life so that your faults and weaknesses are exposed and put to death
Guarded and conditional; based upon others' performance as you seek to get your own needs met	EXPRESSION OF LOVE	Open, patient, and affectionate as you lay your life and agendas down in order to meet the needs of others
Conditional and Distant	SENSE OF GOD'S PRESENCE	Close and Intimate
Bondage	CONDITION	Liberty
Feel like a Servant/Slave	POSITION	Feel like a Son/Daughter
Spiritual ambition; the earnest desire for some spiritual achievement and distinction and the willingness to strive for it; a desire to be seen and counted among the mature.	VISION	To daily experience the Father's unconditional love and acceptance and then be sent as a representative of His love to family and others.
Fight for what you can get!	FUTURE	Sonship releases your inheritance!

Jack and Trisha Frost, Shiloh Place Ministries, PO Box 5, Conway, SC 29528, (843) 365-8990, info@shilohplace.org, www.shilohplace.org. This page can be duplicated if done so in its entirety.

Be

Scripture
Then God blessed them, and God said to them, "Be fruitful and multiply; fill the earth and subdue it; have dominion over the fish of the sea, over the birds of the air, and over every living thing that moves on the earth." - Genesis 1:28

Be still, and know that I am God; I will be exalted among the nations, I will be exalted in the earth! - Psalm 46:10

Description
The Lord commanded His children to "be." This means that everything they would ever do would come out of just being themselves. God would say to you today, "Just be yourself; be who I made you to be. Get so good at being you that you change the world just by being yourself."

Activation
- Draw a picture or write about what it looks like for you to just "be" yourself. Write or draw at least three things that you enjoy or that are an important part of who you are.
  - You can include things like your personality, hobbies, interests, and other areas that you are passionate about.
- Now circle one thing on your paper that you'd like to use to bring the kingdom to earth.
- Write about what that could look like.
  - E.g. If you like playing basketball maybe you'd like to share Jesus with people while you play basketball with them. Maybe you like to cook and you want people to be healed when they eat your food. Maybe you enjoy being in business and you want the people you work with to experience heaven because you are so excellent at your job. If you like kids maybe you can mentor some, do foster care, or even adopt.
- Find a partner and share about who you are and your one specific area where you want to release the kingdom by simply being who God made you to be.

Application
The Lord made each of us as His special children. He does not compare His children or think that some children are better than others. He really does love you just the way He made you to be!

When we love being who God made us to be, we will automatically and intentionally change the world around us. When we really know who we are, we can celebrate others for being who they are.

* Lesson inspired by Pastor Jamey VanGelder, The House Church

Kingdom Mindsets

Then Jesus went about all the cities and villages, teaching in their synagogues, preaching the gospel of the kingdom, and healing every sickness and every disease among the people.
- Matthew 9:35

Salvation is the doorway to God's kingdom, but the kingdom is so much bigger than knowing we will go to heaven when we die, trying to live a good life, or waiting for Jesus to return to earth. We first see the kingdom demonstrated in the Garden of **Eden**. In this place, people lived in perfect relationship with God, each other, and their natural environment. The Garden of Eden shows us God's original plan for what His kingdom would look like on our planet. By learning the principles shown to us in the Garden, we get a picture of what heaven on earth can look like.

As God's chosen people, the nation of **Israel** was supposed to be like Eden again. The Israelites were to be positioned in their land along the main trade routes of their day. There, they would demonstrate the kingdom of God to all who lived in the region and to all who passed through. Israel was to be a place where heaven would be on earth and God would live with His people, and as a result the whole earth would be blessed.

Jesus was the Word made flesh, and He demonstrated what it was like to know the Father and to be a son. Even though Jesus was fully God, He limited Himself to live completely as a human being during His time on earth. In doing so, He modeled what a normal Christian life should look like. Through Jesus' life and teachings we see the kingdom of God demonstrated.

Like another version of Eden, **the Church** is called to release the kingdom of God on the earth. The Church releases the kingdom, but the kingdom of God cannot be contained within the walls or structures of any one church. The true Church of Jesus is not a building, but a group of believers who make up Christ's body on the earth today. Jesus left the earth and put you in charge! **You, ultimately, are His expression of heaven on earth**. The more fully you experience and understand His kingdom, the more naturally you will release it to those around you.

In this section we will look at some practical ways that kingdom people think about God and themselves, and interact with the world around them.

Resources
Teachings by Pastors Jamey and Nicole VanGelder or any House Church leader. iTheHouse.org
When Heaven Invades Earth (or any book) by Bill Johnson or Bethel Church leaders/authors. shop.bethel.com
Teachings from The Mission Church or Mission Church leaders/authors. store.imissionchurch.com

Kingdom Generosity

Scripture
Here is a boy with five small barley loaves and two small fish, but how far will they go among so many? . . Most assuredly, I say to you, unless a grain of wheat falls into the ground and dies, it remains alone; but if it dies, it produces much grain. - John 6:9 (NIV); 12:24

For whoever desires to save his life will lose it, but whoever loses his life for My sake will find it. - Matthew 16:25

But this I say: He who sows sparingly will also reap sparingly, and he who sows bountifully will also reap bountifully. So let each one give as he purposes in his heart, not grudgingly or of necessity; for God loves a cheerful giver. Now may He who supplies seed to the sower, and bread for food, supply and multiply the seed you have sown . . . - 2 Corinthians 9:6,7,10a

But when you give a feast, invite the poor, the maimed, the lame, the blind. And you will be blessed, because they cannot repay you . . . . - Luke 14:13-14a

Description
In the kingdom, whatever we give away multiplies and often returns to us in even greater measure than what we gave away. A little boy had only five loaves and two fish, but when he gave them to Jesus, thousands of people ate and there was more food left over than what he had given to Jesus. The Lord blesses us with a harvest, but in order for that harvest to continue, we need to plant seeds by giving away some of what we have received. We need to discern what to keep and eat as bread, and what to sow as seed so that greater increase can come.

When we have a specific need or desire, we can intentionally begin to sow seed into that area in the lives of others. We can sow seed in prayer, finances, physical items, time, acts of service, or any other areas. In the kingdom we start with receiving, but we need to also intentionally give to others. We give joyfully, not out of pressure or manipulation. We never give to manipulate God or people, trying to get something back.

Activation 1
- Think of the areas of your life where you want breakthrough. If God would do anything for you, what would you want? What would you ask Him for?
- Find a partner and pray that they would get all of those things that you are wanting or needing. Pray for them the same way that you would want someone to pray for you.

Activation 2
- Who do you know that needs something that you have? This could be your time, expertise, a physical item, encouragement, finances, etc. How could you bless them?
- Ask the Lord to show you who to sow into this week and how to bless them.

Application
Intentionally look for ways to be generous to others, even when you are in a place of need yourself. Give to the poor or others who can't pay you back. When others get something that you want, celebrate with them. If someone compliments you on something, what if you gave it to them? Know that when you give something away with a kingdom mindset, what you give actually increases. Look forward to giving, and know that you truly cannot outgive God.

Honor

Scripture

Treat others the same way you want them to treat you. - Luke 6:31 (NASB)

Honor all people. Love the brotherhood. Fear God. Honor the king. - 1 Peter 2:17

Honor your father and your mother, that your days may be long upon the land which the Lord your God is giving you. - Exodus 20:12

Description

Honor can be defined as treating someone with respect, esteem, value, or importance, and regarding them above the common. When we honor people, we should treat others not only as we would want to be treated, but in the same way that we would treat Jesus, Himself. We honor others because we are honorable, regardless of whether or not we think they deserve it. We also honor people for who they are, without getting caught up in who they are not. Honor is something we give to others, not something we ask or demand that others give to us. Looking at how easy or difficult it is for us to honor those in authority over us is often a good way to see how we are really honoring the Lord as our ultimate authority.

Activation 1

- Write down the following and share with a partner if you are in a group:
- How do you live as an honorable person who honors others? What does it look like for you to show honor in your family, to your spouse, at your job, in your school, etc.?
- Are there any people to whom you want to better demonstrate honor? If so, write down their names and what you could do to honor them (give them a gift, pray for them, repent of any bad attitudes you've had against them, etc.).

Activation 2

- Ask the Lord to show you one to three people who He would have you to honor in some way in the next month.
- Ask Him how you could honor them, and write down what comes to mind.
- Spend some time in prayer for those people. If you are in a group, share this with a partner.

Application

As you make it a point to honor those around you, pay attention to the fruit that comes out of those relationships. Recognize that your ability, or inability, to honor others is usually a good indication of your ability to honor the Lord. Think of honor as the currency of heaven.

Resource

Culture of Honor by Danny Silk

Serve Others

Scripture

But he who is greatest among you shall be your servant. - Matthew 23:11

For who is greater, he who sits at the table, or he who serves? Is it not he who sits at the table? Yet I am among you as the One who serves. - Luke 22:27

Jesus interrupted their argument, saying, "The kings and men of authority in this world rule oppressively over their subjects, claiming that they do it for the good of the people. They are obsessed with how others see them. But this is not your calling. You will lead by a different model. The greatest one among you will live as one called to serve others without honor. The greatest honor and authority is reserved for the one who has a servant heart. The leaders who are served are the most important in your eyes, but in the kingdom, it is the servants who lead. Am I not here with you as one who serves you?" - Luke 22:25-27 (TPT)

And He Himself gave some to be apostles, some prophets, some evangelists, and some pastors and teachers, for the equipping of the saints for the work of ministry, for the edifying of the body of Christ. - Ephesians 4:11-12

Description

Jesus, as the Son of God, came to serve us, and told us to follow His example. In the world, people control, manipulate, and dominate others. In the kingdom, all believers lay down their lives to serve other people.

In the church, grace is given to leaders, not primarily to do ministry, but to equip believers to do ministry. This means that all believers are responsible to serve others by changing culture (being apostolic), sharing the good things God has to say (prophesying), telling people about Jesus (evangelizing), caring for others (pastoring), and helping others learn the word of God (teaching). We come to church not only to receive ministry, but to be equipped and serve others. We do not expect our pastors and leaders to do the ministry. Instead, we expect them to equip us, so we can minister and serve.

Activation

- Ask the Lord, out loud, "Lord, how do You want me to serve my _____?"
    - Insert each of the following, one at a time. Listen and write down what He shows you.
        - Spouse, children, parents, co-workers, boss, neighbors, friends, extended family, church, pastors, community, etc.
- Write down and then share what you got with a partner.

Application

Bill Johnson once said, "In the kingdom, we rule with the heart of servants and serve with the heart of kings." No matter how big or important we get, we never outgrow serving. To keep our hearts soft—and especially if we ever feel ourselves getting distracted in pride—we can even look for ways to intentionally serve and go low in ways that no one will ever see.

Connection in Relationships

Scripture
Therefore if you bring your gift to the altar, and there remember that your brother has something against you, leave your gift there before the altar, and go your way. First be reconciled to your brother, and then come and offer your gift. . . . Moreover if your brother sins against you, go and tell him his fault between you and him alone. If he hears you, you have gained your brother. . . Then Peter came to Him and said, "Lord, how often shall my brother sin against me, and I forgive him? Up to seven times?" Jesus said to him, "I do not say to you, up to seven times, but up to seventy times seven." - Matthew 5:23-24;18:15, 21-22

Description
In all of our relationships, it is important that we always stay connected both to the Lord and also to one another. A relationship is like a wooden bridge, and conflict or broken connection can be like a spark on that bridge. If stamped out right away, the connection stays strong. However, if the spark is left alone and not addressed, it can grow until it becomes a fire that can burn down your relational bridge. Jesus taught us that we must both forgive those who have wronged us and also ask for forgiveness from others. When someone wrongs you, sometimes you simply need to forgive them in your own heart. Other times you need to lovingly confront them and make them aware of how their actions affect you so your relationship can be restored. **A good way to do this is by using "I" statements.** Even if we think that someone else may have something against us, we should go to them and make sure that our connection is right. The goal of any confrontation is never to blame, but to restore connection. If someone has hurt you, go directly to them and not to anyone else. If someone else comes to you about something someone else has done to them, direct them back to that person to reconnect. It is good to start by repenting of anything you know you've done, and ask for forgiveness first.

Activation 1
- Ask the Lord to bring to mind any relationship where you have a smoldering spark on your bridge of connection. Do you need to repent or lovingly confront them?
- How and when will you go to this person, or these people, to make this right?

Activation 2
- Role play with a partner to practice reconnecting and then do this in real life later.
- Internally, lean your heart in love towards the person, thank God for them, and bless them.
- Start by asking them to forgive you for anything you know that you have done.
- If you have something against them, confront them using "I" statements and say, "**When you** (specific, non-blaming action) **I felt** (personal emotion: angry, sad, afraid, etc.), **because** (non-blaming, personal reason for your emotions)." You can also add, "**I need to feel** (positive, personal emotion: loved, connected, safe, valued, etc.)."
- Assume that the other person cares about you and wants to make things right. Ask them, "What would you like to do about this?" Or, "Help me understand why this happened."
- If they say they are sorry, tell them, "I forgive you." Also be okay if they do not apologize.

Application
We will need to confront, repent, and ask for and release forgiveness to one another in every single one of our significant relationships. When we bring up issues in a godly way, confrontation doesn't have to be scary or hurtful, but can actually bring us closer together.

Resources
Keep Your Love On by Danny Silk, *Brave Communication* Audio Teaching by Dann Farrelly
Lesson inspired by Pastor Jamey VanGelder, The House Church and Dann Farrelly

Generational Thinking

Scripture

Honor your father and your mother, that your days may be long upon the land which the Lord your God is giving you. - Exodus 20:12

And he will turn the hearts of the fathers to the children, and the hearts of the children to their fathers, lest I come and strike the earth with a curse. - Malachi 4:6

But this is what was spoken by the prophet Joel: "And it shall come to pass in the last days, says God, that I will pour out of My Spirit on all flesh; Your sons and your daughters shall prophesy, your young men shall see visions, your old men shall dream dreams." - Acts 2:16-17

Description

In the kingdom, life flows through honor and each generation needs the other in order to accomplish all that heaven has for us. Fathers and mothers dream dreams that awaken hope in their children. These dreams are big picture ideas, like when someone draws a rough sketch of their dream house on a piece of paper. Sons and daughters have visions that live within the dreams of fathers. These visions are specific, practical ideas that can accomplish the dream, like an architect makes a blueprint for exact instruction on how to build a house. God is the God of Abraham, Isaac, and Jacob. He is a generational God. No one single generation can fully see the kingdom of God advance without connecting their hearts and lives with both the generation that has gone before and the generation coming after them.

Activation 1

- Who are father or mother figures that are in your life directly, or people you respect and admire, even if you do not know them personally? These can be believers or non-believers, and they can even be people who are no longer living.
- What are some of their dreams?
- How can you position your life as a son or daughter and based on the definitions above, have vision within these dreams?

Activation 2

- Who are son or daughter figures in your life? These can be your actual children, or specific people into whom you are pouring (or would like to pour) something of value.
- What dreams do you have that you can share with them, to give them a framework for their vision?

Application

In different areas of our life we are both fathers or mothers, in areas where we are dreaming, as well as sons or daughters, in areas where we have vision. In the kingdom, people can father or mother others older than themselves and be sons or daughters to people who are younger. As you step out in faith and risk, make sure you are connecting your dreams and visions to the generations before and after you.

Resource

*Taken from Pastor Jamey VanGelder's, "Generational Thinking" message, iTheHouse.org

Rest

Scripture

Thus the heavens and the earth, and all the host of them, were finished. And on the seventh day God ended His work which He had done, and He rested on the seventh day from all His work which He had done. Then God blessed the seventh day and sanctified it, because in it He rested from all His work which God had created and made. - Genesis 2:1-3

There remains, then, a Sabbath-rest for the people of God; for anyone who enters God's rest also rests from their works, just as God did from his. Let us, therefore, make every effort to enter that rest . . . - Hebrews 4:9-11a

Description

God made man on day six, and told him to fill the earth and subdue it. Then on day seven, God and man rested. The first day of man was the seventh day of God. From this principle we can see that with God all labor comes out of rest.

Activation 1

If you are busy and on the go, use this simple activation to enter into rest. This works even if you just have 30 seconds, and it can be easily done several times a day.
- Pause for a moment and put your hands out in front of you with your palms facing up.
- Position your heart to receive from the Lord.
- Invite God's presence to come and touch you by saying, "Holy Spirit, come."
- Take a deep breath, close your eyes, and just rest in the Lord.

Activation 2
- Put on some gentle worship (soaking) music and lay down in God's presence.
- Choose to simply let yourself rest in Him.

Activation 3
- Write down some of the things that you need to do (these can be things God has called you to do or just normal tasks). Now, put your list aside.
- Put on a worship song and lay down. Focus on simply resting in God's presence.
- If you think of more things to do, not to do, or to change about your list, briefly write them down or adjust them on your list and then go back to resting.
- When you get up, look at your list again. Ask yourself what it will look like for you to do each of those things from a place of rest.
- After you've done the items on your list, reflect back or write about the difference it made to do those things out of a place of rest.

Application

Everything we do in the kingdom starts with resting and receiving. If you feel yourself becoming stressed or anxious, take a little time to rest in the Lord's presence. Rest doesn't necessarily mean not working. We can be at rest in our hearts and minds even while we are working.

Resource

Soaking in God's Presence manual by Leif Hetland and Paul Yadao

Ministering the Presence of the Lord

Scripture
. . . so that they brought the sick out into the streets and laid them on beds and couches, that at least the shadow of Peter passing by might fall on some of them. Also a multitude gathered from the surrounding cities to Jerusalem, bringing sick people and those who were tormented by unclean spirits, and they were all healed. - Acts 5:15-16

The mountains melt like wax at the presence of the Lord, at the presence of the Lord of the whole earth. The heavens declare His righteousness, and all the peoples see His glory. - Psalm 97: 5-6

Description
Just like Peter's shadow healed people, whatever overshadows us will overshadow those around us, for good or bad. Whatever we are most aware of will be released to those around us. As we stay in a place of being aware of the Lord's presence throughout our day, we allow Him to minister to us and to others in a powerful way. Out of the overflow of all that we receive, we can bless those around us by releasing the presence of the Lord even at times when we cannot minister to someone directly.

Activation 1
- Imagine yourself standing on a mat or a rug that says, "peace." Purposefully stay in that place of peace as you go throughout your day.
- If you begin to experience a lack of peace, take a moment and picture yourself stepping back onto the mat of peace. From this place of being aware of the Lord's peace and presence, go forward with your day.

Activation 2
You can do this exercise with a single partner or by making two lines of people that each face the other (and then have one line step one person to the right to switch partners).
- Stand up and face your partner. You can close your eyes if you want. Imagine yourself standing under a waterfall of the Lord's presence and picture it washing over you. Put your hands out, palms up, and receive all He has for you. Say out loud, "Holy Spirit, come."
- You can even imagine yourself drinking in the Lord's presence, like you would drink something really delicious through a straw.
- Choose one person to be the receiver and one to be the giver. Both partners will lean or position their hearts in love towards the other person.
- The receiver keeps their hands palms up and keeps receiving. Without talking or touching the other person, the giver puts their hands face down over the receiver's hands and, while continuing to receive from the Lord, pictures the waterfall of His presence flowing through them to their partner. The giver can keep their eyes open to see what the Lord is doing.
- Switch partners and talk about what you experienced.

Application
Make it a point to be aware of the Lord's presence throughout your day. Before jumping into prayer or ministry, take a few seconds to ask the Lord how He'd like to minister to the person, and then minister His presence out of a relationship, instead of formula or format.

Impartation

Scripture
For I long to see you, that I may impart to you some spiritual gift, so that you may be established— that is, that I may be encouraged together with you by the mutual faith both of you and me. - Romans 1:11-12

Description
To impart simply means "to give" (Strong's 3330). Paul said he wanted to come to his friends and give them a spiritual gift. What we have in the Spirit we can give to others. When we do this, what we give still belongs to us as well as to the person who has received it. Like Elijah passing on his mantle to Elisha, or the bread and fish multiplying as it was passed out, sometimes what we give actually gets bigger when we give it away. Pastor Bill Johnson says, "We teach what we know, but we impart who we are."

We can lay hands on people and give or impart to them what God has given us. We can also receive impartation by faith, even when people don't lay their hands on us. You do not have to know or communicate what you are imparting. Also, remember what God has done for you and what you carry, to build yourself up to impart with greater faith. Always believe that God will impact the person to whom you are ministering. Ultimately the Lord will work out exactly what gets exchanged between people. Impartation allows people to start at a place that took others a long time to reach. This is also a good way to honor and value not only what the Lord has given us, but also what others around us carry.

Activation 1
- Think about what God has given you or done in your life that you would like to impart.
- Find a partner.
  - Ask if you can put your hand on their shoulder.
  - By faith, declare that what you have in the Spirit you release and impart to them.
- Ask that same person, or a different believer, to impart to you what they have.
  - Lean your heart in honor towards that person, and receive from them by faith.

Activation 2
- Do an impartation tunnel. Have a group of people line up, facing one another, and have another group of people walk between them. People facing the center should place their hands on people's shoulders as they walk by and impart to them what they are carrying.

Application
Regularly, give what the Lord has given you to others. Also, ask others to impart to you. Continue to value and steward what you are carrying and also what you have received.

Kingdom Mindsets - 31

On Earth as it is in Heaven

Scripture
So He said to them, "When you pray, say: Our Father in heaven, Hallowed be Your name. Your kingdom come. Your will be done on earth as it is in heaven."
- Luke 11:2 (Matthew 6:9-10)

But God, who is rich in mercy, because of His great love with which He loved us, even when we were dead in trespasses, made us alive together with Christ (by grace you have been saved), and raised us up together, and made us sit together in the heavenly places in Christ Jesus . . . - Ephesians 2:4-6

Description
Jesus taught His followers to pray that Father God's will would be done on earth the same way that His will is done in heaven. If we ever want to know what God's will is for a situation, we can ask ourselves what that situation would look like in heaven. We don't pray from earth to heaven, asking God to please come down and help us. Rather, we pray with authority from heaven to earth, because we are seated with Christ in heavenly places.

Activation 1
- Draw a big circle on a piece of paper. This represents the world.
- Write down one to three words that represent situations in your life where you need breakthrough.
- Put the piece of paper under your feet, and picture yourself seated in heavenly places.
- From heaven's perspective look around and picture how those situations would look specifically.
- Look down at your paper, and speak the specific reality of heaven into your circumstances.

Activation 2
- Pick one of the above areas. Tell a partner what it is and what it looks like from heaven's perspective.
- Agree together that heaven's reality would come into that situation.

Application
When you find yourself faced with circumstances that are not in alignment with the kingdom of heaven, take a moment to think about, picture, or sense what that situation would specifically look like from heaven's perspective. With that in mind, pray and declare that God's kingdom would come to earth in that situation.

Resource
When Heaven Invades Earth by Bill Johnson

Declarations

Scripture
Death and life are in the power of the tongue, and those who love it will eat its fruit.
- Proverbs 18:21

In the beginning God created the heavens and the earth. The earth was without form, and void; and darkness was on the face of the deep. And the Spirit of God was hovering over the face of the waters. Then God said, "Let there be light"; and there was light. - Genesis 1:1-3

Description
What we say is extremely important. God didn't think creation into being; He spoke it. There is a saying that states, "Words create worlds." What we say really is what we will get, both for good and for bad. We need to **not only think** on the truths of God's Word and His kingdom, but we need to **declare** and **speak** His truths out loud. If our feelings and experiences are not aligned with God's truth, making truth-based declarations will not devalue our feelings or experience. However, it will set a new standard to which our feelings and experiences can rise! As we declare, we change our thinking which can eventually change how we feel and what we experience.

Activation 1
- Ask the Lord to show you one to three areas of your life where He wants to bring breakthrough. Write them down.
- Ask Him what His truth is about each of those areas, from heaven's perspective. Next to each area, write down what comes to mind, along with any Bible verses that you know are related to those areas. For example, if your child has a learning disability, what is true in heaven is that they can learn perfectly.
- Now, write out specific declarations for each area. For example, "My child thinks clearly and can easily concentrate and understand what they are learning."
- Knowing that your words have the power to create, spend time speaking out loud into these situations, declaring truth in faith for things to be created. For example, if you are struggling financially you could declare, "I have more than enough! My finances are so healthy that I always give to the Lord, save, and generously help others."

Activation 2
- Ask the Lord to highlight a Bible verse for an area where you need breakthrough.
- Declare it out loud, making it specific to your life. Listen to your voice as you speak it, and believe in your heart that God's Word will bring it to pass in your life.

Application
Make some kind of positive declaration over yourself every day. Write out specific faith-filled declarations and speak them over yourself regularly. Have your family or friends join you, and speak them together. When you pray, instead of asking God about a situation, declare His truth in that area. For example, instead of saying, "Lord I pray that you would heal this person," say, "I declare healing in Jesus' name." Know that the kingdom is voice activated.

Resources
Books and resources from Igniting Hope Ministries with Steve and Wendy Backlund, IgnitingHope.com, *Decree* by Patricia King, PatriciaKing.com

The Power of the Testimony

Scripture
And they overcame him by the blood of the Lamb and by the word of their testimony... For the testimony of Jesus is the spirit of prophecy. - Revelation 12:11a; 19:10b

Description
A testimony is a story of what God has done in your life. It could be about how you came to know Jesus, as well as all the different ways He is working in your day-to-day life right now. The root of the Hebrew word for "testimony" (Strong's Concordance H5749, `uwd) means "do it again." When we share testimonies, we are actually releasing heaven, changing the atmosphere, and releasing faith for those we are sharing with that God can do that same kind of thing again in their lives.

Activation 1
- Think of a recent testimony of something that God has done in your life.
- Find another person, and share this testimony with them. It is best if you can share something that is both concrete and brief. If you can't think of something that you've experienced, feel free to share a testimony that you know from someone else.

Activation 2
- Ask the Lord to bring to mind a testimony to share with someone else that is also a word of knowledge for them. For example, you might be reminded of the time you or someone else prayed for a person with a specific injury or illness and they were healed, or a relationship that was restored, or a financial breakthrough.
- Share your testimony, and then see if the person needs breakthrough in that same area.

Activation 3
- List one or several areas in your life where you want to experience breakthrough.
- Now purposefully look for testimonies of breakthrough in those areas, reminding yourself that God wants to "do it again" in your life.

Activation 4
- List one or several areas where you want to see breakthrough for those around you.
- Ask God to help you gather testimonies that speak to that specific area. Share them regularly with those who need that breakthrough.

Application
Be intentional about sharing your testimonies with people around you. If there is an area in your family, workplace, or region that needs breakthrough, purposefully look for testimonies in that specific area, and share them regularly. The sower, in biblical times, sowed seed before the plow tilled it into the ground. Likewise, when we sow testimonies, the Lord will come and help get them into the soil of people's hearts.

Resource
Lesson inspired by Pastor Bill Johnson, *The Power of the Testimony* sermon, Bethel Church

What We Focus On We Empower

Scripture
Jesus soon saw a huge crowd of people coming to look for Him. Turning to Philip, He asked, "Where can we buy bread to feed all these people?" He was testing Philip, for He already knew what he was going to do. Philip replied, "Even if we worked for months, we wouldn't have enough money to feed them!" Then Andrew, Simon Peter's brother, spoke up. "There's a young boy here with five barley loaves and two fish. But what good is that with this huge crowd?" "Tell everyone to sit down," Jesus said. So they all sat down on the grassy slopes. (The men alone numbered about 5,000.) Then Jesus took the loaves, gave thanks to God, and distributed them to the people. Afterward He did the same with the fish. And they all ate as much as they wanted. After everyone was full, Jesus told His disciples, "Now gather the leftovers, so that nothing is wasted." - John 6:5-12 (NLT)

Description
Jesus was faced with the big need of over 5,000 hungry people. He and His disciples had only one little boy's lunch. Instead of being overwhelmed by the need, Jesus focused on the provision that He had. When He gave thanks for what He had and started giving it away, what He had multiplied.

Activation
- What is a big need that you have personally (what is your 5,000 hungry people situation)?
- For what can you show gratitude in your situation (your version of the little boy's lunch)?
- Spend time thanking God for those things (like when Jesus gave thanks for the food).
- Out of this place of gratitude, what is one step that you can take to keep moving forward (like when Jesus and the disciples gave out the food)? Now do that this week.

Application
Just like what we focus on we empower, the enemy only has the power that people give him. Jesus took all power and authority from him, so he only has power and authority if people give it to him and empower him. We can choose to empower something that is true (a positive), or something that is a lie (a negative). If we empower it, it will grow, for good or for bad. If you have empowered the enemy by giving him power that belongs to you, repent and picture yourself taking your power and authority back from him.

The next time you find yourself confronted with an impossible problem, look for something good on which to focus and show gratitude. Remind yourself of the miracle from the above story, and expect God to use you to do something big in your situation. As the Lord multiplies what you give to Him, take time to thank Him. Also, keep a running record of what He has done for you!

* Lesson inspired by Pastor Bill Johnson, Bethel Church

Peace Beyond Understanding

Scripture
Be anxious for nothing, but in everything by prayer and supplication, with thanksgiving, let your requests be made known to God; and the peace of God, which surpasses all understanding, will guard your hearts and minds through Christ Jesus. - Philippians 4:6-7

Description
God promises us that His peace will guard us as we stop worrying and gratefully ask Him for help. Sometimes we feel like we have to figure everything out or that we need to fully understand a situation. However, sometimes to have the peace that passes understanding we have to give up our right to understand. When we need to erase fear, the best thing we can do is connect to God and hear from Him.

Once we reach a place of peace and connection with the Lord, it is easier for us to hear from Him, to have confidence that we are making good choices, and to walk in wisdom regarding what to do. Hearing from the Lord does not always mean that He will tell us what to do, but it does anchor us in His presence so that we are able to make decisions out of a place of peace. Peace and connection must always come first.

Activation
- What is an area of your life where you are needing peace?
- Picture Jesus next to you. Ask Him, "Jesus, would you connect with me here?"
- Take some slow deep breaths and rest with Him for a few moments.
- Bring this area before the Lord. Give up your need to have the situation figured out.
    - Picture yourself holding the situation in your hands.
    - Now open up your hands before the Lord, letting this situation go.
- Take enough time to experience true connection with the Lord.
    - Now that you've let this go out of your hands, picture yourself hugging the Lord and Him holding you.
- As you receive more of the Lord's peace and connection, notice how your perspective of your situation changes.
- Ask the Lord, "Lord, what do You want to speak to me," or "What do You want me to know about this situation?"
- Take time to journal about your new perspective and what you hear the Lord telling you.
- Share this with a partner.

Application
When you find yourself feeling anxious about something, come before the Lord and release it to Him until you get to a place of peace and connection with Him. After you are in peace, bring the situation back to the Lord and see if He will give you further wisdom (knowing what to do) or understanding (knowing why to do it) for the situation. Even if you don't feel like you are hearing from the Lord about what to do, simply knowing that you have reconnected with Him will give you courage that you have what it takes to make good decisions as you move forward.

* Lesson inspired by Pastor Bill Johnson, Bethel Church and Pastor Jamey VanGelder, The House Church

Strengthen Yourself in the Lord

Scripture
Then David and the people who were with him lifted up their voices and wept, until they had no more power to weep. And David's two wives, Ahinoam the Jezreelitess, and Abigail the widow of Nabal the Carmelite, had been taken captive. Now David was greatly distressed, for the people spoke of stoning him, because the soul of all the people was grieved, every man for his sons and his daughters. **But David strengthened himself in the Lord his God.** - 1 Samuel 30:4-6

Description
David had just lost everything that was meaningful to him, and he was at risk of being killed. In his time of great distress, David strengthened, or encouraged, himself in the Lord. Out of the place of encouragement, David was able to fight again and regain what was lost. Had he not strengthened himself, he would have stayed in that place of depression and truly lost everything.

There will be times in our lives when things go poorly and the only right choice we can make is to build ourselves up in the Lord. Paul told Timothy to stir up the gift in him (2 Timothy 1:6) and to fight using prophetic words over his life (1 Timothy 1:18). Knowing how to do this regularly will help us keep moving forward and position us to stand in victory.

Activation 1
- Think of an area in your life where you are experiencing difficulty.
- Strengthen yourself in the Lord in that area by speaking life and hope and reminding yourself of past promises or prophetic words. Choose to praise the Lord regardless of how you feel.
- As you strengthen yourself and make declarations over that area, pay attention to how you and your circumstances are affected for the better.

Activation 2
- During a storm in life, increase your worship to a level greater than the storm you face.
- E.g. Have coffee with a friend and do not talk about your problem. As you fellowship with other believers, God will impart grace that will solve the problem.

Application
Have confidence that you will be okay—no matter what happens—because you are able to build yourself up in God and move forward. Trust that as you rightly steward your internal world, the Lord will bring you the answers and wisdom that you need.

Resource
* Lesson inspired by the book, *Strengthen Yourself in the Lord,* by Bill Johnson

Spiritual Warfare

Scripture
"Therefore submit to God. Resist the devil and he will flee from you." - James 4:7

"Behold, I give you the authority to trample on serpents and scorpions, and over all the power of the enemy, and nothing shall by any means hurt you." - Luke 10:9

"For the weapons of our warfare are not carnal but mighty in God for pulling down strongholds, casting down arguments and every high thing that exalts itself against the knowledge of God, bringing every thought into captivity to the obedience of Christ." - 2 Corinthians 10:4-5

Description
While we do not focus on or magnify the devil, we can be aware of his schemes. The enemy is a liar (John 8:44) and an accuser (Revelation 12:10). He accuses us to God (e.g. "Look how bad you are. You should just give up.") and he accuses God to us (e.g. "God is not good and does not love you."). The good news is that we have authority (like a police officer's badge) and power (like a police officer's gun) over the devil and his demons because Jesus defeated the devil when He shed His blood, died, and rose again. Demons often bully, lie, and threaten. They attack identity and can work through other people, whisper thoughts to us that sound like our own, or even manifest more directly. If we agree with them, we open a door and let them into our lives. We can resist the demonic, not agree with their lies, and deny them access to our lives. In areas where we already gave them access we can confess our sin to God, invite the Lord to reveal both the demonic lies and God's truth, speak the truth out loud, and kick the demons out of our lives. Whether we personally experience or see others struggling with strong outward demonic manifestations or subtle thoughts aimed to erode confidence, we can submit to God, resist the devil, and he will flee from us (James 4:7).

Activation
- Speak the following out loud. "Lord please help me to":
  - "**Recognize** one area of my life where I am dealing with spiritual warfare."
  - "**Connect** with You and Your love for me in the middle of this situation (Psalm 23:5)."
  - "**See** any **lies** I am believing here and remember anyone I need to forgive."
    - "I **repent** for believing the lie(s) that _____. I **forgive** _____ for _____."
- "Father, what is Your truth here?" (Declare what He shows you or a Scripture out loud.)
- "I take **authority** over (name the specific situation, thought, demon, etc.) in Jesus' name."
- "I **command** all ungodly spirits (name specific ones the Lord shows you) that gained access to my life through this situation to leave immediately and permanently in Jesus' name."
- "Lord **fill** this area of my life with more of Your presence and truth (Matthew 12:43-44)."

Application
If you don't have much time you can say, "Demon(s) (or spirit of fear, anger, etc.) get out in Jesus' name." Even Jesus was tempted in the wilderness, so just because we are tempted does not mean those things are true or that we need to act on them. Like Jesus, we can see the lies for what they are, speak God's truth, and the enemy will flee. If a thought sounds like you or feels real, but is against God's kingdom, you can reject it. Run to Jesus and connect with Him. Flip the negative thought or feeling and declare the positive, out loud. Take authority, out loud, in Jesus' name. Cast wrong thoughts down and demons out (Matthew 10:8), and change any behavior that let them in (John 5:14). Know that spiritual warfare is never aimed at people, and not all bad things are caused by demons. Always stay more focused on Jesus than the demonic.

Jesus is the Most Normal Christian Who Ever Lived

Scripture
So Jesus said to them again, "Peace to you! As the Father has sent Me, I also send you." - John 20:21

Most assuredly, I say to you, he who believes in Me, the works that I do he will do also; and greater works than these he will do, because I go to My Father. - John 14:12

For what the law could not do in that it was weak through the flesh, God did by sending His own Son in the likeness of sinful flesh . . . - Romans 8:3a

Description
Jesus came to show us how it looked to live as a Son of God on the earth. Everything Jesus did was as a man, who lived in relationship with His Father, with the leading and guidance of the Holy Spirit. If He lived the way He did because He was God, then we would not be responsible to live like Him. However, Jesus came as a man. He faced the same types of trials and temptations as we face, and after His resurrection He gave us access to the same Holy Spirit who dwelt in Him and on Him. Jesus sent us in the same way that the Father sent Him. He told us that we would not only do what He did, but that we would do even greater works!

Activation
- Imagine what it would be like if you woke up every day knowing with all of your being that you were as connected to the Father as Jesus was.
- What would it be like to parent your kids, study in school, go to work, etc. knowing that you could speak the exact truth that people needed to hear, heal all brokenness, multiply areas of lack, etc.?
- Write a list of some of the ways Jesus lived His life and some of the things He did.
- Read over the list again. Imagine living that way too and doing those things in your everyday life.
- Write or share with another person how different your life would look if you really believed you could live your life like Jesus, doing everything that He did, and more.

Application
As you learn about how Jesus lived His life and the works He did, ask the Lord to show you what it will look like for you to live that way every day. Know that you are just as much a son of God as Jesus. Expect and have faith that you can live as powerful of a life as Jesus lived!

* Lesson inspired by Pastor Bill Johnson, Bethel Church

The Light is Green Unless it's Red

Scripture
One day Jonathan said to his armor bearer, "Come on, let's go over to where the Philistines have their outpost. . . Perhaps the Lord will help us, for nothing can hinder the Lord. He can win a battle whether he has many warriors or only a few!" - 1 Samuel 14:1a (NLT)

And Peter answered Him and said, "Lord, if it is You, command me to come to You on the water." So He said, "Come." And when Peter had come down out of the boat, he walked on the water to go to Jesus. - Matthew 14:28-29

Description
Jonathan decided to go pick an unfair fight. He had one sword, was in a low and unsecured place, and decided to climb up to face a large group of armed men in a strong military outpost. God didn't tell Jonathan to fight this battle; Jonathan just decided he wanted to do something to help his people. And, in the end, Jonathan won! There is a saying that goes, **"Faith is spelled R-I-S-K."** Again, Peter didn't wait for Jesus to call him; he came up with the idea of walking on the water and suggested it to Jesus! Then, he took a risk to walk on the water. Even though he soon sank, we celebrate that he took a risk more than we celebrate whether he was successful or not.

Many times, we wait on God to tell us what to do, but He is the One waiting on us. If we have the default attitudes that 1) "the light is green," (i.e. God is for us and supports our choices) and 2) faith is spelled "R-I-S-K," we will take more risks than if we assume that God is telling us "no" before we even start. It is easier to steer a moving car than a parked car. We say, "The light is green unless it's red," because some situations are clearly a red light.

Activation 1
- Draw a large picture of a stoplight with a green light. On the green light area, write down three to five things you'd like to do if you knew that God was giving you a green light.
- Pray through each area, and write down the action steps you could take to start stepping out in each one.
- What is one thing you will do to step into one of these areas this week?
- Share this with a partner.

Activation 2
- If you truly believed that you had a green light from God over your life, what is one specific situation where you would step out and take a faith-filled risk (e.g. pray for someone to be healed, mend a relationship, forgive, prophesy, start a business, etc.)?
- What is one thing you will do to step into that area this week?
- Share this with a partner.

Application
Dream about how you want to make a positive impact in the world. Talk to the Lord about this, but also use courage to take faith-filled risks towards those dreams. Start moving forward, and continue to talk with the Lord as you go. Stay in dialogue with godly people who can encourage, speak truth, and even join you like Jonathan's armor bearer as you go.

The Bible

For the word of God is living and powerful, and sharper than any two-edged sword, piercing even to the division of soul and spirit, and of joints and marrow, and is a discerner of the thoughts and intents of the heart. - Hebrews 4:12

All Scripture is God-breathed and is useful for teaching, rebuking, correcting and training in righteousness, so that the servant of God may be thoroughly equipped for every good work. - 2 Timothy 3:16-17 (NIV)

The Bible, the Word of God, is the foundation for everything in God's kingdom. It shows us who God is, who we are, God's plan for the world, and how we are to live our lives. God wrote the book but He is not fully contained in the Bible. God continues to speak to us today, however everything that we believe, teach, and do must be in alignment with His written Word. Not every situation we find ourselves in will be in the Bible, but the Bible will show us all of the principles that we need to live and walk by with the Lord. Jesus is the Word made flesh (John 1:14). Holy Spirit, who now lives in us, wrote the Bible through people and will teach and lead us into all truth (John 14:26). As we read the Bible we both learn to understand its history and stories and also connect our hearts to the Lord to hear what His voice is speaking to us today. It is important that we have a plan to read the Bible regularly.

The Old Testament is the story of the creation of the world, the fathers of the faith, the law, and the nation of Israel as God's chosen people through which He would reach the world. It follows Israel as they walked with God in times of slavery, wilderness, Promised Land, judges, kings, and captivity. Throughout the Old Testament, different judges or kings ruled the people, various prophets spoke God's truth to them, and psalmists wrote poetry of praise and process to the Lord. During this time, the Lord continually revealed Himself to various people in various ways. In John 14:9 Jesus said that those who saw Him had seen the Father. We read the Old Testament differently when we know Jesus. Jesus did not get rid of the Old Testament, but He did fulfill many aspects of it.

The New Testament tells the story of the life of Jesus, God's son, coming to earth as a man and the perfect revelation of the Father. Jesus gave His life to restore all people to the Father. The New Testament tells the story of the disciples, specifically the Apostle Paul, and many others as they walked with Jesus and formed the early church. The church multiplied as Paul, and others, traveled the region and then wrote letters to different churches and leaders. The New Testament ends with the book of Revelation containing visions of the end of this world and the new heavens and new earth. In this section we will explore ways to connect with God through His Word.

Resources

See the "You Version" Bible app (YouVersion.com) for reading plans, BibleGateway.org for general study, and biblehub.com and blueletterbible.org for detailed word studies.

Relationship with the Author

Scripture
But the Helper, the Holy Spirit, whom the Father will send in My name, He will teach you all things, and bring to your remembrance all things that I said to you. - John 14:26

Now we have received, not the spirit of the world, but the Spirit who is from God, that we might know the things that have been freely given to us by God. These things we also speak, not in words which man's wisdom teaches but which the Holy Spirit teaches, comparing spiritual things with spiritual. - 1 Corinthians 2:12-13

And the Word became flesh and dwelt among us, and we beheld His glory, the glory as of the only begotten of the Father, full of grace and truth. - John 1:14

Description
The Word of God is alive and powerful and as believers we have its author, the Holy Spirit, living inside of us! When we read the Bible we do so in relationship with the Holy Spirit. We ask Him to lead us and help us to understand the Word, both with our minds and in our hearts so that our lives are changed. The more of the Bible we know, the more material Holy Spirit has to work with as He teaches us. (Picture materials and tools to build a home. The more you have to work with the more you can build.) The Bible explains itself. The more we know and compare what the Bible says in different places with what the Bible says in other places, the more we will understand it and grow closer to God.

Even when we do not understand everything we read, we can trust in knowing that it is important to get the Word of God inside of us just as it is important to eat food and drink water. The more we read the Bible the hungrier and thirstier we get for it. It is important that we spend time in the Word even when we do not feel like it. Ideally we will read the Bible every day. Many times as we read we will sense the Lord drawing us to a specific Bible verse or story. When this happens it is important to spend time with the Lord there and see what He wants to share with you. Sometimes you will understand this with your mind and other times you will sense Him doing something in your heart, even if you do not fully understand what you are reading.

Activation
- Ask the Lord out loud, "Lord, what do You want to talk to me about from the Bible?"
- Whatever comes to mind, whether a specific chapter or verse, the story of someone from the Bible, or a specific word like "faith" or "trust," take time to look it up and read it from the Bible. You can look it up online or ask someone to help you find it.
- Read a little before and after the passage and try to understand the context. Whether you understand it or not, keep your heart at rest and connected to the Lord.
- Ask the Lord, "Lord what do You want to show me here?" Write down what He says.
- Now ask Him, "How do You want me to apply this to my life, today?" and write that down.
- Spend time thanking Him for what He showed you and talking to Him about it more.

Application
We read the Bible in relationship with our Father, Jesus, and the Holy Spirit. We expect Him to teach us, lead us, speak to us, and help us grow closer to Him as we read each day.

Connecting with the Bible (SOAP)

Scripture
How sweet are Your words to my taste, sweeter than honey to my mouth! Through Your precepts I get understanding; Therefore I hate every false way. Your word is a lamp to my feet and a light to my path. - Psalm 119:103-105

Description
As we read the Bible regularly it is helpful to have both a specific way that we consistently connect with the Lord through His Word and a daily reading plan. A way to journal and hear God's voice through the Bible as well as a daily reading plan comes from the *Life Journal*. This method called "SOAP" means Scripture, observation, application, and prayer.

Activation 1: SOAP (see the example on page 45)
1. Choose a **S**cripture
   - Pick a passage anywhere from a few verses all the way up to a whole chapter.
   - If possible, read the passage out loud. It can be helpful to write out part of the passage or even mark different words or phrases that stand out to you.
   - **If you are in a group** make sure you all pick the same Scripture. Read the passage out loud then journal the "observe," "apply," and "pray" sections on your own.
   - Pray, "Lord, what are You saying to me today? Please lead and speak to me as I read."
   - As you read, ask the Lord for one thing that He really wants you to focus on.
2. **O**bservation
   - Write down what you observe about the passage. Is there a lesson to learn, an example to follow, a promise to embrace, a way to know Jesus more, etc.?
3. **A**pplication
   - How will I apply what I have read to my life today? What is God saying to me? How will I be different because of reading this? What action will I take? Be as specific as possible.
4. **P**rayer
   - Write out a prayer based on the verse, application, and anything the Lord showed you.

If you are in a group or with a partner:

5. Have each person read out loud what they have written.
6. Share a few short testimonies of what God is doing in your lives.
7. Have each person share one short personal prayer request and close in prayer.

Activation 2: Pick a Plan
- If you don't already have a Bible reading plan go to YouVersion.com, the back of your Bible, or another place, and pick a plan that works for you personally.
- As part of a plan it can be powerful to read the chapter of Proverbs that matches each calendar day and even pick one proverb to rewrite in your own words.
- Share what plan you use or would like to use with a partner.

Application
As we connect with the Lord through His Word daily, it is more important to be consistent, go deep, and be able to personally apply what you read to your life than it is to read a lot. Be okay to go slow and really connect with the Lord. If you ever fall behind in your plan you don't need to go back and read the days you missed, just read the passage for today's date and move forward. Make sure you ask the Lord for one thing He really wants you to focus on from His Word for each day. Consider doing this method with a group once a week.

The Bible - 43

The Three Crosses

Scripture
There were also two others, criminals, led with Him to be put to death. And when they had come to the place called Calvary, there they crucified Him, and the criminals, one on the right hand and the other on the left. . . Then one of the criminals who were hanged blasphemed Him, saying, "If You are the Christ, save Yourself and us." But the other, answering, rebuked him, saying, "Do you not even fear God, seeing you are under the same condemnation? And we indeed justly, for we receive the due reward of our deeds; but this Man has done nothing wrong." Then he said to Jesus, "Lord, remember me when You come into Your kingdom." And Jesus said to him, "Assuredly, I say to you, today you will be with Me in Paradise." - Luke 23:32-33, 39-43

Description
Expanding on the SOAP method from the previous lesson, the three crosses gives even more specific questions to ask for the observation section. This is based on the passage from Luke where Jesus was crucified in the middle with two criminals on either side of Him. One criminal was for Jesus and the other one was against Him. Asking the questions in this method can be especially helpful in group Bible studies because it keeps people focused on applying the Word to their lives and gives them some specific things to think about.

Activation: SOAP and Three Crosses (see the example on page 45)

1. Choose a **S**cripture
- Pick a passage of Scripture. It could be just a few verses but shouldn't be longer than a chapter. If you don't know where to start, use John 15:5-8. If the passage is short, consider writing all or some of it out for yourself. If possible, read the passage out loud.
- Pray, "Lord, what are You saying to me today? Please lead and speak to me as I read."

2. **O**bservation
The Center Cross: This represents Jesus, dying on the cross for us. Ask yourself:
- What does this Scripture teach me about God?
- What do I see in this Scripture that reminds me of myself?

The Left Cross: This represents the criminal who rejected and mocked Jesus. Ask yourself:
- Is there an example in this Scripture that I should avoid?

The Right Cross: This represents the criminal who repented and Jesus promised he would be with Him in paradise. Ask yourself:
- Is there an example in this Scripture that I want to follow?
- Is there a promise for me in this Scripture?

3. **A**pplication
How will I apply what I have read to my life today? What is God saying to me? How will I be different because of reading this? What action will I take? Be as specific as possible.

4. **P**rayer
Pray the passage back to God, talk to Him about what He showed you, confess any sin, commit to live out what you learned, and pray for any other requests you have.

Application
This is a great tool to use for your own study and, especially because the three crosses are so visual, it can be a powerful method to disciple others of all ages.

SOAP Example

Scripture
"I am the true vine, and My Father is the vinedresser. Every branch in Me that does not bear fruit He takes away; and every branch that bears fruit He prunes, that it may bear more fruit." - John 15:1-2

Observation
Jesus, is my source. Father takes things away for my good and helps me focus. Even good things He adjusts to make better.

Application
Today I will look to see what Father is removing and adjusting. With joy I will trust that it is for my good, even if it means letting go of things that I am attached to.

Prayer
"Father, You know it's been hard for me to limit my options and say 'no,' but now I'm reminded that You are already at work in this process! Today please help me to see what you are doing so I can fully let go of what you are taking away and joyfully embrace areas in my life You want to change."

The Three Crosses Example

The Center Cross: This represents Jesus dying on the cross for us. Ask yourself:
- Question: What does this Scripture teach me about God?
  - A: God is good and even when I don't understand, what He does is for my best.
- Question: What do I see in this Scripture that reminds me of myself?
  - A: I am helpless to make anything happen on my own. I can't prune myself or take off my branches, but I can have a good attitude while the Lord does this.

The Left Cross: This represents the criminal who rejected Jesus. Ask yourself:
- Question: Is there an example in this Scripture that I should avoid?
  - A: Later on in John 15 it warns what will happen if I do not abide in Jesus. I need to make sure that I keep Him as my source and don't try to live my life in my own strength.

The Right Cross: This represents the criminal who repented. Ask yourself:
- Question: Is there an example in this Scripture that I want to follow?
  - A: I want to keep abiding in Jesus and receiving life from Him.
- Question: Is there a promise for me in this Scripture?
  - A: As I stay connected to the vine, I will grow into what I am to become. I don't have to have everything figured out, but can trust the Father to bring adjustments to my life as needed. As I live each day with Him, I will have life and grow.

Bible Study

Scripture
These were more fair-minded than those in Thessalonica, in that they received the word with all readiness, and searched the Scriptures daily to find out whether these things were so.
- Acts 17:11

Description
The Bible covers over 4,000 years of history, contains 66 books, and was written through dozens of people from many different language backgrounds. Its writing styles range from history and genealogies to prophecy, poetry, parables, letters, and more. The people to whom it was originally written lived in cultures and had experiences that differ from ours today. While the Word of God is alive and powerful to speak to us in our personal lives today, we also want to understand what it meant to its original audience. One way to do this is to think about what we are reading, and to ask ourselves a lot of questions about the passage. Then we keep reading and looking in the Bible to try to find those answers. Another way to deeply understand the Bible is to look up what specific words meant in their original language, and where a word or topic appears throughout the Bible.

Activation 1: Ask Questions
- Pick a full or partial chapter of the Bible. If you don't know where to start, read John 1.
- Ask these questions about the passage and write down your answers.
- If you are in a group setting, you can discuss each question together. Or write down your answers and then share with the whole group later. Feel free to write down, mark, or circle key words or phrases in the passage that stand out to you.
  - **Who** – Who wrote this? Who is it talking about? Who was it written to? Who is talking?
  - **What** – What is happening? What does it mean? What did it mean to the people it was written to? What happened just before and after this? What stands out to you? What kind of writing is this (e.g. a letter, prophecy, poetry, parable, genealogy, etc.)?
  - **When** – When did this happen? When will this happen? When was it written?
  - **Where** – Where did this happen? Where will this happen? Where was this written? Where else in the Bible does it talk about something similar?
  - **Why** – Why is this being communicated? Why is this important? Why was this written?
  - **How** – How did this happen? How will this happen? How can you apply this to your life?

Activation 2: Study a Topic
- Pick a word, topic, or person that stands out to you from the passage you just read (e.g. faith, hope, Moses, etc.), and use the websites listed under Resources on page 41 to look up where else that word is in the Bible and even what it meant in its original language. Read as much as you can about this word, topic, or person to understand what the Bible has to say about it.

Application
As you read the Bible in a relationship with the Lord, seek to understand what you read by asking questions and looking up other verses. This lets the Bible interpret itself. Be patient and know that you will not be able to have all of your questions answered. Sometimes it can help to read other resources to understand the Bible, but we should always start with the Bible itself. Remember to ask the Lord how He wants you to live out what you learn.

46 - Kingdom Culture School of Ministry

Pray the Bible

Scripture
I have rejoiced in the way of Your testimonies, As much as in all riches. I will meditate on Your precepts, And contemplate Your ways. I will delight myself in Your statutes; I will not forget Your word. - Psalm 119:14-16

Description
When it comes to meditating on the Bible we can read it, rewrite what we have just read, sing the passage, and say it out loud. We call this "read it, write it, sing it, say it." One powerful way to meditate on the Word of God is to pray it back to the Lord. You can do this with just about any Bible passage. As you pray, you can ask the Lord questions or pray to apply the passage to a specific part of your life. It works best to do this out loud and while moving (this will help you stay focused and keep your mind from wandering).

Activation 1
- Pick a passage you enjoy or use the one below and pray it back to God out loud.

   For this reason we also, since the day we heard it, do not cease to pray for you, and to ask that you may be filled with the knowledge of His will in all wisdom and spiritual understanding; that you may walk worthy of the Lord, fully pleasing Him, being fruitful in every good work and increasing in the knowledge of God; strengthened with all might, according to His glorious power, for all patience and longsuffering with joy; giving thanks to the Father who has qualified us to be partakers of the inheritance of the saints in the light. He has delivered us from the power of darkness and conveyed us into the kingdom of the Son of His love, in whom we have redemption through His blood, the forgiveness of sins. - Colossians 1:9-14

- Practice doing this for different lengths of time. Start with five minutes but continue to add time. Don't be afraid to repeat the passage over and over again and see what new insight you get each time you pray.
- You can also gather a series of shorter verses around a set topic that you read or memorize and pray them back to the Lord

Activation 2
- Pray for yourself or another person by putting your or their name in the passage that you pray out loud back to the Lord.

Application
Not only does praying the Bible help us to learn it better, but when we pray the prayers of the Apostles and other believers in Scriptures, it teaches us how to pray. When we pray through the revelations of who God is from the Bible, it helps us know the Lord in a deeper way.

Resource
Praying the Bible: The Book of Prayers by Stacey Campbell

Biblical Meditation

Scripture
This Book of the Law shall not depart from your mouth, but you shall meditate in it day and night, that you may observe to do according to all that is written in it. For then you will make your way prosperous, and then you will have good success. - Joshua 1:8

Description
Some religions meditate by emptying their minds, but Christians meditate by filling their minds with the truth. Meditating on the Bible can look like saying a passage to yourself in your mind or out loud, over and over again. The more you think about and say the passage the more it will get inside of you, until it becomes a part of who you are. It is natural then to pray the verse back to the Lord, over yourself, or for another person or situation. In the Catholic tradition there is a way of reading Scripture called "Lectio Devina," which is Latin for, "Sacred Reading." This way of meditating on Scripture has helped many people encounter the Lord for hundreds of years.

Activation
- Pick a short passage of Scripture, just a couple of verses, and write it out on a separate piece of paper.
- If you don't know where to start, use this passage:
  The Lord is my shepherd; I shall not want. He makes me to lie down in green pastures; He leads me beside the still waters. He restores my soul; He leads me in the paths of righteousness for His name's sake. - Psalm 23:1-3
- Read the passage a total of four times. Read the passage out loud, but quietly, and without emphasizing any phrase or word above another. Pause to see what the Lord shows you.
- You can do this exercise individually or in a group. If you are doing this in a group, have a different person read the passage each time and then take turns sharing with each other what you saw at each step.

Steps for Lectio Devina
1. Read the passage out loud and look for **one word or phrase** that stood out to you.
2. Read the passage out loud and ask the Lord where this passage **connects with your life** right now.
3. Read the passage out loud and ask what God is calling you to **do in response.**
4. Read the passage out loud and **rest in silence.**

Application
Meditating on small sections of Scripture can help you slow down. By doing this, you are able to see the importance of every word and phrase, and allow them to impact your life. It is good to memorize a verse so that you can easily call it to mind throughout the day and say it back to yourself. Regularly take time to meditate on and ponder God's Word. You can even think of it like eating a really good meal. The more bites you take the more flavor you can enjoy and savor. Just like eating in the natural, meditating on the Word will feed and change you!

Creative Bible Studies

Scripture
Deal bountifully with Your servant, that I may live and keep Your word. Open my eyes, that I may see wondrous things from Your law. - Psalm 119:17-18

Description
The Bible is a living book that we understand because we are in relationship with the Author. As we explore creative ways to interact with the Scriptures we get to know the Lord in new, fun, and powerful ways. When we interact with the Bible we will get more out of it if we not only read it, but also write it, pray it, sing it, say it, etc.

Activation 1: Write
- Rewrite a passage in your own words.
- Write a one sentence summary of the passage.
- Pretend that you are in the middle of the passage and write a story about it.

Activation 2: Draw
- Draw a picture of a Bible story or passage of Scripture.
- You can draw a single picture or many pictures of the story unfolding, like a comic strip.
- Feel free to draw bubbles over people's heads and write what they are saying or thinking.
- You can also draw yourself into the picture as you imagine which of the different characters you would be and what the story would look like from their perspective.

Activation 3: Sing or Dance
- Write a song, create music, and/or a dance about a Bible passage.

Activation 4: Act
- Act out a Bible passage with some friends.
- After you are done, talk with each other about what you learned through acting it out.

Application
Coming to the Bible from a fresh perspective can help us experience it in a deeper way and learn truths we may have missed simply by reading it. Creative Bible studies are also wonderful ways to connect the generations together.

Foundational Principles

Therefore, leaving the discussion of the elementary principles of Christ, let us go on to perfection, not laying again the foundation of repentance from dead works and of faith toward God, of the doctrine of baptisms, of laying on of hands, of resurrection of the dead, and of eternal judgment.
- Hebrews 6:1-2

Now is the time for us to progress beyond the basic message of Christ and advance into perfection. The foundation has already been laid for us to build upon: turning away from our dead works to embrace faith in God, teaching about different baptisms, impartation by the laying on of hands, resurrection of the dead, and eternal judgment. So with God's enablement we will move on to deeper truths.
- Hebrews 6:1-3 TPT

Jesus is the door we enter through so we can live in the kingdom. In our new life in Christ, the Bible lists several foundational principles that are important for every believer to know. Even if we think we are already familiar with these topics it is still good to remind ourselves of them and even learn them well enough that we could share them with others.

In this section we will look at a few of the elementary principles listed in Hebrews 6 and other areas of Scripture.

Repentance

Scripture
"The time is fulfilled, and the kingdom of God is at hand. Repent, and believe in the gospel." - Mark 1:15

. . . and that repentance and remission of sins should be preached in His name to all nations, beginning at Jerusalem. - Luke 24:47

Repent therefore and be converted, that your sins may be blotted out, so that times of refreshing may come from the presence of the Lord. - Acts 3:19

What shall we say then? Shall we continue in sin that grace may abound? Certainly not! How shall we who died to sin live any longer in it? . . . Therefore do not let sin reign in your mortal body, that you should obey it in its lusts. And do not present your members as instruments of unrighteousness to sin, but present yourselves to God as being alive from the dead, and your members as instruments of righteousness to God. For sin shall not have dominion over you, for you are not under law but under grace. What then? Shall we sin because we are not under law but under grace? Certainly not! Do you not know that to whom you present yourselves slaves to obey, you are that one's slaves whom you obey, whether of sin leading to death, or of obedience leading to righteousness? . . . For the wages of sin is death, but the gift of God is eternal life in Christ Jesus our Lord. - Romans 6:1-2, 12-16, 23

Description
Repentance means to change your mind, turn around, and go in a different direction than you were going before. When we truly repent, turn away from our sin, and live in faith towards God, we leave our sin behind. More than simply feeling sorry, repentance means our hearts and minds are now different and, therefore, our behavior will change as well. If we simply feel bad but do not change, we have not repented. If we know the right thing to do and do not do it, we are walking in iniquity and there will be consequences for our actions. It is one thing if we are actively working with the Lord to overcome an area of sin, wounding, or weakness in our life. However if we are simply willfully living in sin and trying to justify that it is okay because God still loves us, we have not yet repented of that sin. Even though we live under grace and not the law, we need to both live and teach true repentance that does not allow us to embrace sin.

Activation
- Have you truly repented of all areas of sin in your life?
- Ask the Lord to show you any areas where you still need to fully repent.
- Bring each area before the Lord, one at a time. Ask Him to not only forgive you but to also show you how to think differently.

Application
When you face that area of sin in your life moving forward, pay attention to your thoughts and make sure they line up with the Word of God. As you renew your mind, your feelings will begin to change and, as a result, you will naturally act differently. While we never walk in shame, make it a point to not tolerate any area of sin in your life and to quickly bring any known sin before the Lord and actively walk in repentance. Tell a trusted friend about these areas so they can encourage you as you walk in repentance.

Water Baptism

Scripture

Or do you not know that as many of us as were baptized into Christ Jesus were baptized into His death? Therefore we were buried with Him through baptism into death, that just as Christ was raised from the dead by the glory of the Father, even so we also should walk in newness of life. For if we have been united together in the likeness of His death, certainly we also shall be in the likeness of His resurrection, knowing this, that our old man was crucified with Him, that the body of sin might be done away with, that we should no longer be slaves of sin. - Romans 6:3-6

He who believes and is baptized will be saved; but he who does not believe will be condemned. - Mark 16:16

Description

Baptism is both a picture of our salvation and an actual experience of being baptized into Jesus' death and resurrection. We go down into the water, where our old self dies and is forever buried. Our resurrected self comes up into new life. Anyone who is old enough to have a personal relationship with Jesus should be baptized. Being baptized is a public declaration of our faith and our new life in Christ.

Different churches and cultures may have different traditions or requirements associated with baptism. There are many New Testament accounts of entire households being baptized at once. Since baptism represents what happens at salvation, an individual should be old enough to make a free-will choice to give their life to Jesus in order to be baptized. Many parents choose to dedicate their children to the Lord as infants and when the children are old enough they can choose salvation and then baptism for themselves.

Activation

- If you have been baptized, think back to your baptism and reflect on what God did in your life during that time.
- If you have not been baptized, reflect on what has kept you from getting baptized and what you would like to do to be baptized in the future.
- Journal your reflections and/or share with a partner.

Application

In the New Testament, believers were often baptized immediately after salvation by being fully immersed in water by a fellow believer. The Bible does not give any instructions on who can and cannot baptize another person. Many people choose to be baptized by a pastor or elder in the church but a person can be baptized even by a friend who is a believer. Scripturally, you only need to be water baptized once.

Local Church

Scripture

And let us consider one another in order to stir up love and good works, not forsaking the assembling of ourselves together, as is the manner of some, but exhorting one another, and so much the more as you see the Day approaching. - Hebrews 10:24-25

Now when they had come and gathered the church together, they reported all that God had done with them, and that He had opened the door of faith to the Gentiles. - Acts 14:27

So, being sent on their way by the church, ... - Acts 15:3a

Therefore take heed to yourselves and to all the flock, among which the Holy Spirit has made you overseers, to shepherd the church of God which He purchased with His own blood. - Acts 20:28

Description

All believers, worldwide and throughout time, are a part of the Church and body of Christ. In addition to this, we should each be a part of a local church, or body of believers, in our area. Within our local church we are accountable to other believers for our choices and actions, submit to the authority of our leaders, volunteer with our time, and have fellowship in community with other believers.

While it is wonderful to receive from conferences, internet-based resources, teachings from various ministers, and even different Christian groups, these things do not replace the local church. A local church is a place where we are committed not only spiritually, but also relationally and financially. While believers are called to "go into all the world," we must also have a place where we are each rooted and grounded, a place to know and be known, and a place to serve and receive from. As we go out, our local church can send us and then receive us back.

The church is not a perfect place, as any place that has people will also have some messes. We cannot get all of our needs met from our church, and we may at times be hurt by the people in our community. It is still our responsibility to stay rightly connected, walk in forgiveness, and be a contributing part of a local church community.

Activation

- If you are a part of a local church, spend some time both thanking the Lord for how He has blessed you there and also praying for your leaders and church community.
- If you are not a part of a local church, talk to the Lord about why that is (walking through forgiveness of previous churches if necessary) and what you will do to get connected to a local congregation.

Application

Be a healthy, contributing member of a local church. Use your gifts and talents to serve within your church, and gather with other believers from your church to serve your community and even other nations.

Giving

Scripture
So let each one give as he purposes in his heart, not grudgingly or of necessity; for God loves a cheerful giver. - 2 Corinthians 9:7

Description
There are three main kinds of giving listed in the Bible.

Tithes are the first 10% of our income, and they go to support our local church. Tithe means 10%.
- *And all the tithe of the land, whether of the seed of the land or of the fruit of the tree, is the Lord's. It is holy to the Lord. - Leviticus 27:30*

Offerings are what we choose to give above and beyond our tithe and can be given anywhere.
- *For all these out of their abundance have put in offerings for God, but she out of her poverty put in all the livelihood that she had. - Luke 21:4*

Alms are given in secret to the poor, and are a loan to the Lord.
- *And a certain man lame from his mother's womb was carried, whom they laid daily at the gate of the temple which is called Beautiful, to ask alms from those who entered the temple . . . - Acts 3:2*
- *So when you give to the needy, do not announce it with trumpets, as the hypocrites do in the synagogues and on the streets, to be honored by others. Truly I tell you, they have received their reward in full. But when you give to the needy, do not let your left hand know what your right hand is doing, so that your giving may be in secret. Then your Father, who sees what is done in secret, will reward you. - Matthew 6:2-4 (NIV)*
- *Whoever is kind to the poor lends to the Lord, and He will reward them for what they have done. - Proverbs 19:17 (NIV)*

Because the tithe doesn't actually belong to us, many believers have found that if they didn't give it to the Lord, it would seep out of their income on its own. However, when they did tithe, their expenses often decreased or provision came in other areas.

Activation
- Write out a list of what you are currently giving in each of the three areas listed above.
- Spend some time talking to the Lord about your current giving, and ask Him if He has anything He wants to share with you.
- Write out a list of what you would ultimately like to be able to give in each area in the future.
- What steps will you take to get from where you are now to where you want to be?

Application
Everything we own already belongs to the Lord. By giving, we are simply investing back into His kingdom some of the good things He has given to us. Giving generously not only helps others, but also anchors our hearts in the reality of heaven. We do not give out of compulsion. We also do not give to God to get something back from Him (e.g. We do not give money so that we will be healed or blessed). In giving, not only are others blessed and provided for, but we are reminded of the Source of our provision.

Communion

Scripture

And as they were eating, Jesus took bread, blessed and broke it, and gave it to them and said, "Take, eat; this is My body." Then He took the cup, and when He had given thanks He gave it to them, and they all drank from it. And He said to them, "This is My blood of the new covenant, which is shed for many." - Mark 14:22-24

And as they were eating, Jesus took bread, blessed and broke it, and gave it to the disciples and said, "Take, eat; this is My body." Then He took the cup, and gave thanks, and gave it to them, saying, "Drink from it, all of you. For this is My blood of the new covenant, which is shed for many for the remission of sins." - Matthew 26:26-28

For I received from the Lord that which I also delivered to you: that the Lord Jesus on the same night in which He was betrayed took bread; and when He had given thanks, He broke it and said, "Take, eat; this is My body which is broken for you; do this in remembrance of Me." In the same manner He also took the cup after supper, saying, "This cup is the new covenant in My blood. This do, as often as you drink it, in remembrance of Me." For as often as you eat this bread and drink this cup, you proclaim the Lord's death till He comes. - 1 Corinthians 11:23-26

Description

Jesus told us that communion is His body and blood that was shed for us. He instructed us to share this meal with other believers in remembrance of what He did for us. Communion can be taken in many different ways, both individually and in groups.

Activations

Below are a few ideas for how to take communion:

- Since Jesus paid for our sins and sicknesses in His body and by His blood, focus on receiving and releasing forgiveness and healing to one another in communion.
- Gather with others and take turns remembering Jesus by sharing testimonies of what He has done in your life. Eat bread and drink from the cup each time someone shares or simply treat your entire meal as communion.
- Communion is similar to the Jewish betrothal ceremony where a future bride would drink a cup to say, "I do" and set herself apart in preparation for her bridegroom. Position yourself as the bride of Christ, and as you take communion renew the covenant between yourself and Jesus. Commit to fully live for Him each day.

Application

Take communion regularly on your own and with other believers. Let this practice minister grace to you and draw you closer to Jesus as you remember that He gave His life for you.

Laying On of Hands

Scripture
And when Simon saw that through the laying on of the apostles' hands the Holy Spirit was given, he offered them money. - Acts 8:18

They will take up serpents; and if they drink anything deadly, it will by no means hurt them; they will lay hands on the sick, and they will recover. - Mark 16:8

As they ministered to the Lord and fasted, the Holy Spirit said, "Now separate to Me Barnabas and Saul for the work to which I have called them." Then, having fasted and prayed, and laid hands on them, they sent them away. - Acts 13:2-3

Therefore I remind you to stir up the gift of God which is in you through the laying on of my hands. - 2 Timothy 1:6

Description
We can lay hands on people for healing, impartation, to appoint them to leadership (if we have the authority to do so), to release the Holy Spirit, or to give them a spiritual gift.

When we put our hands on people, we always want to do so in an appropriate way. It is good to ask someone if we can touch them and get their permission first. The shoulder is usually a good place to put your hand. If they need physical healing, you can also have them put their hand where it hurts, then put your own hand on top of their hand. Be careful about men laying hands on women and women laying hands on men. Be sensitive to what is honoring and appropriate in various cultures and settings.

Activations
- Partner up with someone. Ask if you can put your hand on their shoulder and release the Holy Spirit to them.
- Find a different partner. Ask to put your hand on them (remember to ask first) and release a spiritual gift to them. You can give them anything that you have.
- Find someone who is sick. Ask if you can put your hand on their shoulder and release healing to them.

Application
Regularly experience the kingdom of God being released through your hands!

Praise and Worship

Scripture
Enter into His gates with thanksgiving, and into His courts with praise. . . I will call upon the Lord, who is worthy to be praised; So shall I be saved from my enemies. . . Give unto the Lord the glory due to His name; Worship the Lord in the beauty of holiness.
- Psalm 100:4a; 18:3; 29:2

And I fell at his feet to worship him. But he said to me, "See that you do not do that! I am your fellow servant, and of your brethren who have the testimony of Jesus. Worship God! For the testimony of Jesus is the spirit of prophecy." - Revelation 19:10

Description
When we come before the Lord it is good to begin with thanksgiving. We praise God by expressing how much we admire Him and approve of Him. Some words for praise in the Bible mean to shout, to dance with abandon, or to declare His goodness. Some words for worship in the Bible mean to bow low, to lay down flat, or literally to kiss the hand of one who is highly honored. Worship involves us bowing low before the Lord, not only physically, but in our hearts.

We are created with a desire to worship something greater than ourselves. If not aimed in the right place we can direct this worship towards possessions, other people, idols, angels, our jobs, or even our problems or ourselves. While we can be thankful for, praise, and approve of others for who they are and what they've done, only the Lord is worthy of worship.

Activation 1 - Thanksgiving
- Come before the Lord and tell Him how thankful you are for Him, for who He is to you, and for what He's done in your life.

Activation 2 - Praise and Worship
- Practice praising and worshiping God with your body. You can take it slow or do this quickly. Try using music, singing/speaking words, using only shouts/sounds, and/or silence.
- Lift your hands high up in the air, jump up and down, dance, and even shout wildly.
- Continue moving and dancing but slow down. This can even be a choreographed dance.
- Slow your body down so you are standing in one place and just lift your hands up high.
- Stand still and lift your hands out at waist level.
- Stand and bow or bend forward.
- Kneel down but stay tall with your torso. Raise your hands and then bring them to your side.
- Kneel down and lay down on the ground with your torso. Put your hands out in front of you.
- Lay completely flat on the ground with your hands and feet stretched out.

Application
We praise and worship with our voices, bodies, and most importantly, our hearts. By using our bodies and voices we give God our full selves. We do not need to be in church or have music to praise and worship God. We can always connect with Him in our hearts, even as we go throughout our daily lives.

Resources
The Power of Praise and Worship by Terry Law, BethelMusic.com/WorshipSchool

Personal Health

Beloved, I pray that you may prosper in all things and be in health, just as your soul prospers.
- 3 John 1:2

Now may the God of peace Himself sanctify you completely; and may your whole spirit, soul, and body be preserved blameless at the coming of our Lord Jesus Christ.
- 1 Thessalonians 5:23

The Lord loves us and wants every part of who we are, body, soul, and spirit, to experience His kingdom. While our spirits are seated with Christ in heavenly places, our souls (mind, will, and emotions) still need to be renewed and continually healed from past and present hurts.

The enemy and his kingdom primarily have influence in our lives to the extent that we have unforgiveness or believe his lies, and through doing so, we invite his kingdom to rule within us. When we see what lies we are believing, repent of them, forgive, and receive God's truth, we will be set free.

Similar to physical healing, some inner healing happens instantly and some can take time. Just like we need to care for our physical bodies, we also need to take care of our souls. Jesus paid for all of our sins and sicknesses on the cross, and He also paid for all the brokenness and pains of our souls.

As you go on a process of healing and maintaining personal health, connect with the Lord and allow Him to bring up what He wants you to deal with. He will give you wisdom for how, and in what settings, to step into freedom. You may also want to visit an inner healing ministry (see list below) or professional Bible-based counselor to have others help you. Just like we believe in supernatural healing but still need to take care of our bodies and can visit doctors, we also know we are to walk in wholeness of soul but still need to steward our thoughts. It can be good to seek help from others if we are needing more freedom and healing than we can find on our own.

In this section, we will go over a few simple exercises to help us forgive others, receive freedom, and walk in health in our inner world.

Resources
Inner Healing Ministries: Sozo (BethelSozo.com) (Many lessons in this section are based on this ministry), Immanuel (ImmanuelApproach.com), and Restoring the Foundations (RestoringTheFoundations.org)
Incredible Life Makeover: Step-by-Step Transformation to Wholeness by Julie Court (NewLife4Today.com)
Loving on Purpose, the ministry of Danny Silk (LovingOnPurpose.com)
The Supernatural Power of Forgiveness and other resources by Jason Vallotton (jasonvallotton.com)
Books and resources by Dr. Caroline Leaf (DrLeaf.com)

Forgiveness

Scripture
Then Peter came to Him and said, "Lord, how often shall my brother sin against me, and I forgive him? Up to seven times?" Jesus said to him, "I do not say to you, up to seven times, but up to seventy times seven." - Matthew 18:21-22

And forgive us our sins, for we also forgive everyone who is indebted to us. - Luke 11:4a

Description
Unforgiveness is like drinking poison and hoping someone else gets sick; it hurts us much more than it hurts the other person. As Christians, we are required to forgive others. Forgiveness isn't a feeling; it is a choice. Forgiveness means we release someone from the debt that they owe us and choose not to hold their sins against them anymore.

Forgiveness does NOT mean we have regained trust with the person who hurt us, that we continue to allow them to hurt us, or that the person doesn't still have consequences for their actions. We may still need to be healed of what the person did to us and may also need to set healthy boundaries with them so we do not continue to be hurt in the future. Whenever we realize we have unforgiveness, we can forgive, bless, and take authority.

Activation 1
Say all of the following points out loud. If you are in a group, you can be very quiet and just pray under your breath but still speak these out loud.
- Ask the Lord, "Lord, who do I need to forgive?"
- Say, "For what do I need to forgive them?"
- **Forgive**: Pray specifically for each person and situation, "Lord I forgive ___(name)___ for (specific hurtful actions). I renounce the lie that You, Lord, would ever treat me this way."
- **Bless**: Now pray for each person saying, "Lord I bless (name) with (specific blessings)."
- **Take Authority:** Say, "By the authority Jesus gives me, I command all ungodly spirits that gained access to my life through these people or situations to leave immediately and permanently."
- Pray, "Holy Spirit, come fill and have lordship over all areas affected by this situation."

Activation 2
- Write a list of people who you need to forgive and what they did to hurt you.
- Now tear up the list into very small pieces and throw them in the air like confetti.
- Celebrate with Jesus that you have fully let go of these circumstances, and receive His joy!

Application
If you have anything against another person you must forgive them, because Jesus commanded us to do so. Sometimes, we forgive someone and then later realize we still have more things that we are holding against them. The good news is that you can forgive an endless amount of times! You don't necessarily need to tell the person about your process of forgiving them, as this can actually hinder your relationship with them. However, walk through complete forgiveness to the extent that you no longer need anything from the other person. Then, allow the Lord to help you decide if you should tell them that you no longer hold anything against them or have forgiven them for a specific situation, or if you should pursue reconciliation to mend your relationship.

Release Mercy, and Forgive Sins

Scripture
"If you forgive the sins of any, they are forgiven them; if you retain the sins of any, they are retained." - John 20:23

Mercy triumphs over judgment. - James 2:13b

Confess your sins to one another, and pray for one another, that you may be healed. The effective, fervent prayer of a righteous man avails much. - James 5:16

Then behold, they brought to Him a paralytic lying on a bed. When Jesus saw their faith, He said to the paralytic, "Son, be of good cheer; your sins are forgiven you." And at once some of the scribes said within themselves, "This Man blasphemes!" But Jesus, knowing their thoughts, said, "Why do you think evil in your hearts? For which is easier, to say, 'Your sins are forgiven you,' or to say, 'Arise and walk'? But that you may know that the Son of Man has power on earth to forgive sins"—then He said to the paralytic, "Arise, take up your bed, and go to your house." And he arose and departed to his house. - Matthew 9:2-7

Description
Jesus had the power to forgive sins and said that we would do the same and even greater works than He did. He told us that if we forgive anyone they are forgiven and if we do not forgive them they are not forgiven (John 20:23). Just like Jesus, we have the power to forgive people and release them from their sins. We can release people from their sins, even if they have not sinned against us personally. When someone tells us what they have done we can verbally and intentionally release them from their sin and the weight of guilt that they are carrying.

Activation 1
- Find a partner, look them in the eye, and tell them, "I release mercy over you. I do not hold your sins against you. Be forgiven and released."

Activation 2
- As you are talking with your friends and family, if others share something negative that they have done and are having a hard time letting go of, take time to verbally tell them that they are forgiven.
- If you hear of injustices happening, even to people you do not directly know, speak mercy and forgiveness over them.

Activation 3
- Wash someone's feet as an act of releasing mercy and that their sins are washed away.

Application
You can release forgiveness and mercy to others without even needing to know what they did specifically. Release mercy and forgiveness over yourself regularly. You can also speak mercy and forgiveness over others when you take communion with them.

* Lesson Inspired by Pastor Jamey VanGelder, The House Church

Release and Receive

Scripture

The Lord has done great things for us, and we are glad. Bring back our captivity, O Lord, as the streams in the South. Those who sow in tears shall reap in joy. He who continually goes forth weeping, bearing seed for sowing, shall doubtless come again with rejoicing, bringing his sheaves with him. - Psalm 126:3-6

So Jesus answered and said, "Assuredly, I say to you, there is no one who has left house or brothers or sisters or father or mother or wife or children or lands, for My sake and the gospel's, who shall not receive a hundredfold now in this time—houses and brothers and sisters and mothers and children and lands . . ." - Mark 10:29-30a

Description

Many times we need to release things to the Lord that we aren't supposed to be carrying: wrong ways of thinking, hurtful memories, etc. When we give these things to God, we need to make sure we are getting filled up again and getting something back in exchange.

Activation

- Cup your hands like a bowl in front of you.
- Think of everything in your life that you don't want to carry anymore. Using your imagination, put those things (ideas, struggles, people, etc.) in your hands. You can take as much time as you want and you don't have to tell anyone what those things are.
- If you're leading another person in this, have them look up at you when they're done.
- Now picture Jesus standing in front of you. He has a big smile on His face. His hands are like a bowl underneath your hands.
- When you're ready, open up your hands and picture yourself releasing all of the things in your hands into Jesus' hands.
- Now put your hands back together again like a bowl in front of you.
- Ask Jesus out loud, "Jesus, now that I've given You all these things, what do You want to give me in return?"
- Picture or sense what He is giving you or putting in your hands.
- Share with another person and/or write down what He showed you.

Application

Whenever you need to give something to the Lord, ask Him what He wants to give you in return. Sometimes doing a physical act to release and receive something helps our heart to engage and have faith for what the Lord is doing. This activation is very helpful if someone is coming to you for prayer but what they really need is to let some things go and hear from the Lord for themselves.

Finding the Root

Scripture
You will know them by their fruits. Do men gather grapes from thornbushes or figs from thistles? Even so, every good tree bears good fruit, but a bad tree bears bad fruit. A good tree cannot bear bad fruit, nor can a bad tree bear good fruit. - Matthew 7:16-18

See, I have this day set you over the nations and over the kingdoms, to root out and to pull down, to destroy and to throw down, to build and to plant. - Jeremiah 1:10

But He answered and said, "Every plant which My heavenly Father has not planted will be uprooted." - Matthew 15:13

Description
Every fruit in your life is fed by a root system. When you have bad fruit, it is better to take out the entire tree by its roots than it is to constantly pick the bad fruit that will only keep growing back.

Activation
Pray the following out loud:
- "Lord, show me an area of my life that You want to heal."
- Now ask the Lord, "Lord, what is the root of this area? When was the first time I felt this way or experienced this situation? What is its source?"
  - You may have specific memories or even general situations come to mind.
  - Even if what comes to mind does not seem related, take a moment and look at it together with the Lord.
- Ask Him, "Lord, what lie did I believe when this happened?"
  - Ask the Lord, "Lord please forgive me for believing the lie that _____."
  - By doing this you are taking out the plant by the root.
- Now ask Him, "Lord, what is the truth?"
  - Say, "Thank you Lord for showing me the truth that _____." Declare it over yourself.
  - This plants a new root system in place of the old one.
- Now say, "I command all ungodly spirits that gained access to my life through this situation to leave immediately and permanently in Jesus name."
  - Taking authority clears out any remaining weeds or bad seeds.

Application
If you come upon a situation in your day-to-day life where you have a really big reaction to a small situation, recognize there may be a bigger root system there. For example, if your kid spills milk and you get very angry and yell at them, your big emotional response to a small situation is telling you that there is more going on than just spilled milk. The problem isn't the kid or the milk, the problem is something else (a root) in your life, from which God can set you free.

Personal Health - 63

Healthy Living

Scripture

Or do you not know that your body is the temple of the Holy Spirit who is in you, whom you have from God, and you are not your own? For you were bought at a price; therefore glorify God in your body and in your spirit, which are God's. - 1 Corinthians 6:19-20

So you shall serve the Lord your God, and He will bless your bread and your water. And I will take sickness away from the midst of you. No one shall suffer miscarriage or be barren in your land; I will fulfill the number of your days. - Exodus 23:25-26

Description

It is great to be healed. It's even better to not need to be healed because we are living a healthy lifestyle. Walking in divine health is a combination of making healthy practical choices and receiving supernatural grace for health from the Lord. When the children of Israel came out of Egypt there was not one sick person in their midst (Psalm 105:37). Later, God told them that they would stay healthy and have no miscarriages or barrenness. Even after forty years of walking around the wilderness, their shoes did not wear out, and even their animals were extremely healthy. If divine health was the reality of the Israelites hundreds of years before Jesus, how much more can we live in divine health after the cross?

Activation

- On a scale of 0-10, with 0 being so unhealthy you're about to die and 10 being 100% perfect health, what number would you give yourself in the following health areas?
  - Physical ____, Nutritional ____, Exercise ____, Sleep ____, Hydration ____, Sexual ____
  - Mental ____, Emotional ____, Spiritual ____, Work ____, Rest ____, Play/Hobbies ____
  - Relational ____, Marriage/Family ____, Financial ____, Time Management ____
  - Any other areas you want to write in _____, _____
- One at a time for each area, ask the Lord these questions. Listen and write down what He shows you.
  - "Lord, what do You want to speak to me about my _____ (physical, exercise, mental, etc.) health?"
  - "Are there any lies I'm believing about myself in this area that I need to repent of?"
  - "What truth do You want to speak to me in this area?"
  - "What strategy do You want to show me to walk in divine health in this area?"
  - "Who can I share this strategy with who can help keep me accountable?"
- Take a few minutes, close your eyes, and picture how your life would be different if you and your family were always healthy. Ask the Lord to give you faith to believe for this.
- Share these things with a partner.

Application

At every meal take time to speak a blessing over your food. Know that it is the blessing of the Lord that keeps you healthy and not only your self effort. Expect the Lord to give you strategy and wisdom for how to practically take care of yourself. Choose to do what you know is right by making lots of small healthy choices every day.

Outreach

"All authority has been given to Me in heaven and on earth. Go therefore and make disciples of all the nations, baptizing them in the name of the Father and of the Son and of the Holy Spirit, teaching them to observe all things that I have commanded you . . ." - Matthew 28:18b-20a

For I am not ashamed of the gospel of Christ, for it is the power of God to salvation for everyone who believes, for the Jew first and also for the Greek. - Romans 1:16

So then neither he who plants is anything, nor he who waters, but God who gives the increase. Now he who plants and he who waters are one, and each one will receive his own reward. - 1 Corinthians 3:7-8a

As believers it is our privilege to reach out and share the Good News of Jesus with the world around us. We desire to share our faith with others and that starts by simply loving the person in front of us, seeing them as Jesus sees them, and looking at them with a heart of compassion. As we talk with each person we want to connect with them, help them to encounter the Lord, and invite them to move closer to God. Look to see what Holy Spirit is doing and how far you can take the conversation to help the person journey further into the kingdom.

Connect: Take time to value the person you are talking with for who they are without having an agenda. This can look like simply starting up and staying in a conversation (any conversation, not just a spiritual one), complimenting them, introducing yourself, asking them questions, and/or seeing what they need prayer for. Sincerely listen to them, seek to really understand what they are telling you, and draw them out by asking them more questions.

Encounter: We owe the world an encounter with the living God. Help the person you are connecting with to experience God's love, presence, power, goodness, voice, or healing. This can look like praying for them, ministering the Lord's presence, healing the sick, prophesying words of life and encouragement, or manifesting whatever gift of the Spirit will bring that person closer to the Lord.

Invite: Invite the person to know Jesus on a deeper level. This can look like sharing your salvation testimony or a recent testimony, sharing the Gospel, and inviting the person to receive all that Jesus has for them. If the opportunity is there, ask the person if they would like to surrender their life to Jesus. Be ready for them to say, "Yes," and pray with them.

Salvation introduces people to Jesus and is their first step to a new life in the kingdom. People getting saved is just the beginning, and as they grow as believers, we are to walk alongside and help disciple them. We are excited and unashamed to share the good news of the kingdom whether we are sowing, watering, or bringing in the harvest. As we are comfortable being our authentic selves and demonstrating the kingdom, we will find that many people want to join us on the journey.

Resources

CompassionToAction.com / GGA.global / LoveSaysGo.com / NoPlaceLeft.net / 4CMCInternational.org / t4tonline.org / PowerAndLove.org / YWAM.org / IrisGlobal.org

Fear Not

Scripture
Therefore I remind you to stir up the gift of God which is in you through the laying on of my hands. **For God has not given us a spirit of fear, but of power and of love and of a sound mind.** *Therefore do not be ashamed of the testimony of our Lord, nor of me His prisoner, but share with me in the sufferings for the gospel according to the power of God, who has saved us and called us with a holy calling, not according to our works, but according to His own purpose and grace which was given to us in Christ Jesus before time began, but has now been revealed by the appearing of our Savior Jesus Christ, who has abolished death and brought life and immortality to light through the gospel . . . - 2 Timothy 1:6-10*

Description
Sometimes we are so afraid to reach out to others that we do nothing. Or we put so much pressure on ourselves to get someone saved or healed that we feel intimidated and do not even say, "hello" to them. We as believers have power, love, and a sound mind.

The ways of the enemy often have short-term gain and long-term pain. God's ways often require sacrifice or doing hard things at the beginning (pain) but lead to long-term gain. When making any decision we can "fast forward" to what the effects of this decision will be down the road. In outreach we can ask ourselves, "What is the worst that could happen?" or "What is the best that could happen?" If the worst that could happen is feeling foolish, the person saying, "no," or not liking us, that really isn't so bad. If the best that could happen is their life, family line, and city are forever changed because they encountered Jesus in a powerful way, it is worth the risk to reach out to them!

Especially when talking with strangers, it is okay if we feel a little awkward sometimes. However, our confidence will increase when we know how much Father loves us, we receive His love for another person, and start a conversation with a heart to sincerely connect with and love them.

Activation
- Write down or share with a partner some people who are on your heart to reach out to. These can be specific people you know or general groups like homeless people, neighbors, telemarketers, etc.
- Write down or share some ways that you can be your authentic self and connect with these people to love them well. For those you know maybe it's sending a text or social media message, inviting them to a meal, or visiting their home. For those you don't know maybe it is a simple phrase or question you can say to them to start a conversation.
- For each way you listed to connect, write down or share what is the best and the worst thing that could happen if you do these things.

Application
Whenever it is on your heart to reach out to someone or to do something good but you feel afraid, ask yourself, "What is the worst or best thing that could happen?" Don't overthink it but take courage to go and connect with others in love and trust the Lord to touch them.

Connect

Scripture
Then He said to them, "The harvest truly is great, but the laborers are few; therefore pray the Lord of the harvest to send out laborers into His harvest." - Luke 10:2

A woman of Samaria came to draw water. Jesus said to her, "Give Me a drink." For His disciples had gone away into the city to buy food. Then the woman of Samaria said to Him, "How is it that You, being a Jew, ask a drink from me, a Samaritan woman?" For Jews have no dealings with Samaritans. Jesus answered and said to her, "If you knew the gift of God, and who it is who says to you, 'Give Me a drink,' you would have asked Him, and He would have given you living water." . . . And at this point His disciples came, and they marveled that He talked with a woman; yet no one said, "What do You seek?" or, "Why are You talking with her?" The woman then left her waterpot, went her way into the city, and said to the men, "Come, see a Man who told me all things that I ever did. Could this be the Christ?" Then they went out of the city and came to Him. - John 4:7-10, 27-30

Description
Before we can be a part of bringing in the harvest we first need to connect with the harvest. This can be as simple as striking up a conversation with another person, sincerely valuing them for who they are, being present to listen to them, and asking good questions. As we connect in a normal conversation we can ask the Lord to show us how He would have us demonstrate His kingdom to them. This can look like sharing a testimony, giving a prophetic word, providing comfort, or a number of other ways. One very practical way to connect with people and help them encounter God is to ask how you can pray for them.

Activation 1 (Strike up and stay in a conversation)
- Start up a conversation with someone that you don't know and introduce yourself to them.
- Be yourself. Ask a couple of questions to draw them out. Typically, start with non spiritual questions. You can ask them how they are, what has been the best part of their day/week, if they know what their name means, or any question that helps you connect with them.
- Be intentional to truly love, listen, be present, and stay sincerely interested in what they are telling you.

Activation 2 (Add value)
- Ask the Lord how you can add value to this person. Continue talking with them but add in some encouragement, prophecy, a testimony, comfort, or more questions to draw them out.

Activation 3 (Offer prayer, and pray there)
- As you continue your conversation find a way to ask them, "How can I pray for you?"
- Take a moment and pray for them right there, in a non-religious way. Keep your eyes open, as if you are continuing your conversation. If you want to put a hand on them, make sure to ask them first.

Application
Practice doing this on a regular basis. After praying for the person, be open to sharing your testimony, prophesying, healing, sharing the Gospel, and leading them to the Lord.

Outreach - 67

How Can I Pray for You?

Scripture
"The prayer of a righteous person is powerful and effective." - James 5:16b (NIV)

Description
Most people are open to prayer and it is one of the most powerful ways to both connect with them and help them encounter the Lord. You can say, "I like to pray for people," and then ask, "How can I pray for you?" Then pray for them briefly and immediately, in a non-religious way, as part of your conversation. You can also ask people if they have any pain in their body or if they need healing for anything physically. Oftentimes people are in pain but don't think to mention it.

When praying you don't need to close your eyes, bow your head, or even touch the person (but if you do touch them, please ask first and only put your hand in an appropriate place). Simply keep your eyes open like you are having a normal conversation and transition the conversation into talking to the Lord about what the person just requested. This is especially important when you are talking with people who are busy working, because you want to honor their time and not draw unnecessary attention to them. One way to think about this is to "practice" praying for others how you would pray for a busy non-Christian politician in a public government office. If we get used to praying this way all the time, we will easily be ready to pray for people both in and outside of church in our daily lives.

Activation 1
- Find a partner, introduce yourself to them, and then ask, **"How can I pray for you?"**
- **Without touching them, closing your eyes, or even changing your tone, pray a one minute prayer or declaration over them.**
  - If they need healing simply say, "Pain go in Jesus' name! (List their specific need here) be healed in Jesus' name." Then have them test it out if they can, to see if it is better.

Additional Activations
- **Restaurants and Grocery Stores**
  - Practice saying this to a partner and then to your server in a restaurant when you order or a cashier at the grocery store when you buy food. "I am going to pray for the food when it comes (or when I make it at home). When I do, how can I also pray for you?"
  - If the person is open you can even pray for them quickly right then or follow up with them after you pray and share anything good you sensed for them during prayer.

- **Phone Calls and Sales**
  - Find a partner and pretend they are a telemarketer, door-to-door salesperson, or a phone support person. Tell them, "I know this may seem strange and doesn't have anything to do with what we just talked about, but I like to pray for people. How can I pray for you?"
  - The next time you talk to a person like this on the phone or in person, ask them this question at the end of your time and then pray for them briefly right there.

Application
Regularly ask people how you can pray for them and then pray for them immediately in a non-religious way. Do this with your family, friends, and co-workers as well as with strangers. The more you incorporate asking to pray for others into your daily routine, the more open doors you will find to share the Lord with people. Don't be afraid to ask even high level leaders how you can pray for them (as most people are trying to get something from them and rarely ask what they can do for them).

Feeling God's Presence

Scripture

And heal the sick there, and say to them, "The kingdom of God has come near to you." - Luke 10:9

For the kingdom of God is not in word but in power. - 1 Corinthians 4:20

Then Jesus went about all the cities and villages, teaching in their synagogues, preaching the gospel of the kingdom, and healing every sickness and every disease among the people. - Matthew 9:35

Description

People are hungry to experience God and His goodness. The Gospel, which is Good News, should look like practical and powerful good news to those who receive it. Many times people will be powerfully touched, healed, etc. first and then come to know Jesus afterwards. One example of this is in John 9, when the blind man was healed by Jesus and only later found out who Jesus was and believed in Him. In addition to healing and also prophesying over people, having people experience God's presence is a great way for them to encounter His kingdom.

Activation

- Find a partner and introduce yourself to them. Ask them if they'd like to feel God. On the streets you can ask people: "Have you ever felt God before?" "Would you like to feel God?" "Would you like to feel something really cool?"
- When they say, "yes," have them put out their hands with their palms facing up.
- Put your hands over their hands but don't touch their hands.
- Tell them to repeat after you and then say, "Holy Spirit, come."
- As they say it, release Holy Spirit on them and keep your eyes open to see what happens.
- Ask them what they are feeling or sensing (maybe heat, weight, or tingling).
- Pray that God would increase that.
- Let them know that it is God's presence touching them.
- If they don't feel anything just encourage them by telling them how much God loves them!
- Ask them if they know Jesus. If they don't, share the Gospel and lead them to the Lord.
- You can try this by yourself as well. Just put your hands out and say, "Holy Spirit, come." Then wait and see how the Lord touches you.

Application

Expect God to touch people. Always give someone an encounter with the Lord and not just information. Find someone this week and ask them if they want to experience God's presence. If they say, "yes," then do this exercise with them.

Your Salvation Testimony

Scripture
And they overcame him by the blood of the Lamb and by the word of their testimony. - Revelation 12:11a

For the testimony of Jesus is the spirit of prophecy. - Revelation 19:10b

One of the two who heard John speak, and followed Him, was Andrew, Simon Peter's brother. He first found his own brother Simon, and said to him, "We have found the Messiah" (which is translated, the Christ). And he brought him to Jesus. - John 1:40-42a

Description
Sharing what Jesus has done in your life is a powerful way to preach the Gospel. You are the only Jesus people may ever meet and the only Bible that they may ever read. No one can argue with your experience. When you share what Jesus has done in your life it gives others hope for what He could do in their life! It's important that we are able to share briefly and also keep the conversation going by asking, "Do you have a story like that?"

When sharing your salvation testimony think about what your life was like before Jesus, how you got saved, and what your life has been like after you accepted Jesus. If you don't remember what your life was like before Jesus because you have known Him as long as you can remember, that is a powerful testimony in and of itself. If you had a time where you fell away and rededicated your life to Jesus, you can also share about that experience.

Activation 1 (15 Second Testimony)
- Look at the sample on the next page and write your own 15 second testimony. Practice sharing this out loud with several people. You can use different words depending on who you talk to. Keep it VERY brief. Make sure to ask the person you are talking to if they have a story like this and listen to what they say.
- "There was a time in my life when I (two words that describe your life before Jesus)."
- "Then I surrendered my life to Jesus."
  - (If you are in a pagan society you can add, "and made Him my one and only God.")
- "Now I (two words that describe what your life has been like after Jesus)."
- Ask the other person, "Do you have a story like that?" Listen to what they say and continue the conversation.

Activation 2 (1-3 Minute Testimony)
- Write out your testimony in 1-3 paragraphs, using a few more details. See the example on the next page.
- Find a partner and practice sharing your testimony with them in 1-3 minutes.

Application
Know your testimony and be ready to share it and the Gospel message. Assume that people will want to hear it and that they will be open to receiving the Lord. Be prepared to adjust what you share and how you share it depending on your audience and how much time you have. Ask the Lord to show you who you can share your salvation testimony with this week.

15 Second Testimony

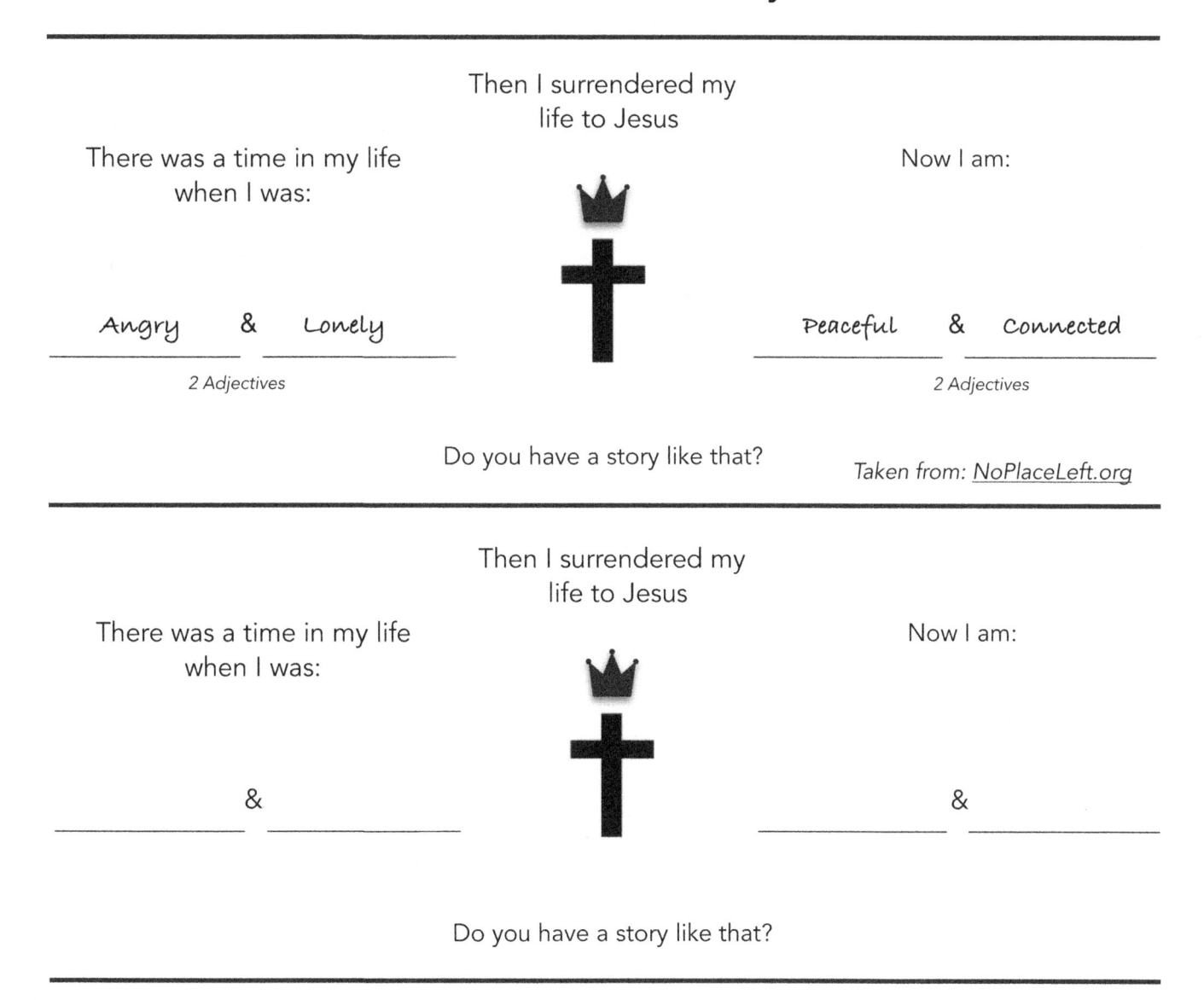

There was a time in my life when I was:

Then I surrendered my life to Jesus

Now I am:

Angry & Lonely

2 Adjectives

Peaceful & Connected

2 Adjectives

Do you have a story like that?

Taken from: NoPlaceLeft.org

There was a time in my life when I was:

Then I surrendered my life to Jesus

Now I am:

___ & ___

___ & ___

Do you have a story like that?

1-3 Minute Testimony Example

While I had a good home and a family who loved me, I still had pain and brokenness. I experienced a lot of anger, fear, and rejection growing up, so I thought God was angry with me and far away. I knew about God from church but always thought religion was a bunch of overwhelming rules to follow that I could never keep up with. When I was thirteen years old I visited a church with my older brothers, who had recently surrendered their lives to Jesus. When I walked into the service I felt the presence of God. The pastor talked about how Jesus loved me and wanted to connect with me. He said that Jesus gave His life to pay for all the bad things I had done so that I could be forgiven and experience a loving relationship with Him. I learned that I could make a choice to receive this gift and that day, I prayed a prayer to surrender my life to Jesus. Every day of my life since then, Jesus has led me. Over time He healed my parents' marriage and restored our family. He set me free from the deep pain I carried in my heart. Jesus transformed me from being the shyest, most socially awkward person I had ever met to being a confident person who knows how much I am loved. He moved me from isolation into community and continues to journey with me in my process every day. Do you have a story like that?

Sharing the Gospel

Scripture
For I am not ashamed of the gospel of Christ, for it is the power of God to salvation for everyone who believes, for the Jew first and also for the Greek. - Romans 1:16

Description
It is very important that we understand salvation from the Bible for ourselves and that we are ready to share this message with others in whatever simple way will be the most helpful for them. We do not necessarily need to share Bible verses with other people to explain salvation to them, however John 3:16 is the most known Bible verse in the world and can be a wonderful verse to memorize and use to share the Gospel. We can also use simple key words and even actions to help ourselves remember the Gospel message (and sometimes these are helpful ways to share with others as well). Look at the verses, symbols, and actions on the next page and then practice sharing them in the activations below.

Activation 1
- Read through the entire next page and meditate on the verses.

Activation 2
- Read the bold phrases out loud, several times, and do the actions with each one.
- Share this with a partner.

Activation 3
- Put the bold phrases into your own words and practice them with and without the actions.
- Share this with a partner.

Activation 4
- Memorize John 3:16 and use that verse as a way to share the Gospel with your partner.

Activation 5
- Practice sharing your 15 second testimony with a partner, ask them if they have a story like that, and then transition into sharing the Gospel with them.

Activation 6
- Ask your partner, "Do you know for sure if you died tonight that you would go to heaven? Would you like to know for sure?" Then share the Gospel with them.
- If a person ever says, "Yes I do know for sure," then ask them, "How do you know for sure?" And have a dialogue with them.

Activation 7
- Say to a partner, "Do you want Jesus? Pray with me now."

Application
Become as comfortable as possible in simply and briefly sharing the Gospel. Be open to taking a conversation as far as it can go and share the Gospel in your own words. Make sure to clearly invite people to accept Jesus and ask if they would like to do that right now.

A Simple Way to Share the Gospel

LOVE

Say: "God loves us and wants us to be with Him."

Action: Hug yourself.

For God so loved the world that He gave His only begotten Son, that whoever believes in Him should not perish but have everlasting life. - John 3:16

* It is important to start with love and establish that God is a good, loving God.

SIN

Say: "When we do bad things, we walk away from God."

Action: Put your hand out and look away, like you are rejecting someone.

For all have sinned and fall short of the glory of God. - Romans 3:23
For the wages of sin is death, but the free gift of God is eternal life in Christ Jesus our Lord. - Romans 6:23

* This is important because it shows the problem we have and also that we are the ones who are rejecting God because of our choices. We don't necessarily have to use the word, "sin" but can talk about doing bad things.

GIFT

Say: "Jesus, God's son, lived a perfect life, died on the cross, and rose from the dead to pay for all the bad things we have done."

Action: Put your hands out like Jesus dying on the cross.

But God demonstrates His own love toward us, in that while we were yet sinners, Christ died for us. - Romans 5:8
For by grace you have been saved through faith, and that not of yourselves; it is the gift of God, not of works, lest anyone should boast. - Ephesians 2:8-9

* This is important because we cannot work hard enough to save ourselves. We are not perfect, but Jesus was. It is also important to say that Jesus <u>rose from the dead</u> because that is why He has the power to save us.

CHOICE

Say: "This leaves us with a choice. We can reject what Jesus has done and stay separated from God forever. Or we can accept what Jesus has done for us, surrender our lives to Him, turn away from the bad things we have done, and make Jesus our one and only God. Would you like to do that right now?"

Action: Put your hand on your chin and look like you are making a big decision.

If you confess with your mouth Jesus as Lord, and believe in your heart that God raised Him from the dead, you will be saved; for with the heart a person believes, resulting in righteousness, and with the mouth he confesses, resulting in salvation. - Romans 10:9-10

* This is important because it shows us we are responsible to make a choice. It also talks about repentance (turning away from the bad things we have done) and surrendering our lives to Jesus (making Him our only God - or you can say, "making Him our Lord and Savior."). You can also say that if we are separated from God forever the Bible says that we will go to hell, but if we surrender our lives to Him we will not only go to heaven when we die, but we will experience eternal life right now. It is good to talk about rejecting God first and accepting Jesus second. Finally, make sure to ask the person if they want to do this right now.

Prayer For Salvation

Scripture
That if you confess with your mouth Jesus as Lord, and believe in your heart that God raised Him from the dead, you will be saved; for with the heart a person believes, resulting in righteousness, and with the mouth he confesses, resulting in salvation. - Romans 10:9-10

Description
After we share the Gospel and people are ready to receive Jesus, we get to pray with them to invite the Lord into their life and help them know how to live for Him. We can use the same way that we shared the Gospel with a person to pray with them. Notice that a simplified version of this prayer goes A, B, C or Admit, Believe, Choose (or Confess).

Activation 1
- Read the next page. Speak the "say" sections out loud and do the corresponding actions.

Activation 2
- Practice leading a partner to the Lord by having them repeat the phrases on the next page after you. Make sure to give them short phrases to say and then wait for them before moving on to the next phrase.

Activation 3
- Have a partner repeat a salvation prayer after you, using your own words.
- Here are some more sample prayers you can use:
  - **Super Simple Prayer:** "Lord save me, forgive me, heal me, and fill me!"
  - **Prayer for Salvation:** "Jesus, I believe that You died on the cross for my sins and rose from the dead. I receive Your love and forgiveness and surrender my life to You. Thank You that I am now a child of God. Please help me to live for You all of my days. Amen."

Activation 4
- Practice adding in a prayer for forgivingness and/or the baptism of the Holy Spirit. Have your partner repeat out loud after you.
- **Prayer for Forgiveness** (which will bring deliverance):
  - "Lord, I choose to forgive all those who have hurt me (including myself) and declare mercy over their lives. I release them from all of their sin." (If there are other areas of addiction or pain that person is in, they can pray to release those things to the Lord.)
- **Baptism of Holy Spirit:** "Holy Spirit, I ask You to come in power and fill me right now."

Application
When we can be our authentic selves and be confident in our ability to share the Gospel with others, then as the Lord leads we will be excited about opportunities to share the Good News of Jesus. If we have an idea of where we can take a conversation when someone is ready to receive the Lord, we can be more comfortable and present to focus on loving the person in front of us and then leading them to Jesus.

A Simple Salvation Prayer

LOVE - <u>T</u>hank

Say: "THANK YOU God that You love me."

Action: Hug yourself.

SIN - <u>A</u>dmit

Say: "I ADMIT that I have walked away from You."

Action: Put your hand out and look away, like you are rejecting someone.

GIFT - <u>B</u>elieve

Say: "I BELIEVE, Jesus, that You died on the cross and rose from the dead for me."

Action: Put your hands out like Jesus dying on the cross.

CHOICE - <u>C</u>hoose

Say: "I CHOOSE to turn away from the bad things I've done, surrender my life to you, and make You my God."

Action: Put your hand on your chin and look like you are making a big decision.

A Couple of Extra Items You Can Pray

FORGIVE

Say: "I forgive all those who have hurt me."

FILL

Say: "Holy Spirit, fill me now."

Four Ways to Grow

Scripture
And they continued steadfastly in the apostles' doctrine and fellowship, in the breaking of bread, and in prayers. - Acts 2:42

Day after day, in the temple courts and from house to house, they never stopped teaching and proclaiming the good news that Jesus is the Messiah. - Acts 5:42 (NIV)

Description
After leading someone to the Lord it is important to share with them how they can continue to grow as a believer in Jesus. Here are four ways to grow that we can share with every new believer.

1. **Pray**: Prayer is talking to God. Listen for God to talk back to you and follow His leading.
2. **Bible**: Get a Bible and read it regularly. A good place to start is in the book of Mark or John.
3. **Church**: Go to a local church that preaches Jesus and connect with other believers.
4. **Share**: Tell others about Jesus and what He has done for you. You can also do what Jesus did by loving people, healing the sick, etc.
5. **Good**: (If you want, you can add in a fifth way to grow.) Do good. Begin to do good in every way that you know to do and trust that God will use it to bring His kingdom.

Activation 1
- Read through the four ways to grow and practice saying them out loud with the hand motions.

Activation 2
- Share with a partner the four ways to grow using the hand motions.
- Share with a partner without using the hand motions.

Application
After you lead someone to the Lord, make it a point to share these ways to grow with them. If they don't have a Bible, help them get one. Also make sure to get their contact information and help them get connected to a local church or invite them to a church or Bible study that you know about.

Four Ways to Grow

PRAY
Say: "Prayer is talking to God. Listen for God to talk back to you and follow His leading."

Action: Hands together, praying.

BIBLE
Say: "Get a Bible and read it regularly. A good place to start is in the book of Mark or John."

Action: Hands together, palms up, like a book.

CHURCH
Say: "Go to a local church that preaches Jesus and connect with other believers."

Action: Shake hands to show connection with other people.

SHARE
Say: "Tell others about Jesus and what He has done for you. You can also do what Jesus did by loving people, healing the sick, etc."

Action: Hands by your mouth as if you are announcing something.

Discipleship

Scripture

Then Jesus came to them and said, "All authority in heaven and on earth has been given to me. Therefore go and make disciples of all nations, baptizing them in the name of the Father and of the Son and of the Holy Spirit, and teaching them to obey everything I have commanded you. And surely I am with you always, to the very end of the age."
- Matthew 28:18-20 (NIV)

Description

After leading someone to the Lord you are responsible to help them be discipled. At the very least, get their contact information and help them get connected to a church or Bible study in their area. At best, invite them to a small group or Bible study in your home where you will disciple them along with several other people.

This is a model you can use to disciple people. It is used by church planters in over 50 nations. It is designed to not only be a Bible study, but also to allow time to share testimonies and help people take action to apply what they are learning to their lives immediately. The idea is that anyone could study the Bible on their own, but only in community can we help one another to practice what we are learning and keep each other accountable for how we are living it out. This method does not tell you what to study. We recommend you take people through basic core kingdom beliefs and that you use the SOAP and/or Three Crosses Bible study method mentioned earlier in this book. You can also use this book to cover different topics.

- **Look Back:** Care for one other, pray for each other, share testimonies, talk abut how it went living out what you learned last week, and encourage one another to share the Gospel.
- **Look Up:** Read and study the Bible together. You can use the SOAP and/or Three Crosses method from the Bible section of this manual.
- **Look Forward:** How will you live out what you have learned? Is there anything you can practice with someone in the group?

Spend equal amounts of the time on each part above. It will be necessary to consistently use all three parts in order for the Bible study participants to grow and spread the Good News throughout the community. However, when time is limited you may need to shorten your Bible study time.

Activation
- Read through the discipleship model on the next page.
- Are you currently discipling anyone?
- Are there people in your life who you could begin to disciple? If so, who are they?
- If you were to start a discipleship group, what would it look like? Where would you meet? Who would you invite? Who could help lead it with you?

Application

As we lead people to the Lord, they are like newborn babies just entering into the world. The work is not finished, rather their process has only just begun. Whether we raise them up ourselves or we help them connect with others, it is important to follow up with them as soon as possible after they receive Jesus and help them to grow in the Lord. Ideally we should help someone get connected to a church or Bible study within 24 hours after they receive the Lord.

Look Back
Testimonies

- How did you apply what you learned last week?
- What testimonies do you have?
- Who did you share Jesus with?

Look Up
Word

- Study the Bible

Look Forward
Goals and Practice

- How will you apply what you learned to your life this week?
- Who will you share Jesus with?
- Is there anything you need to practice with someone here?

Look Back (1/3 of time)

Care and Pray

Ask each person:
- How are you?
- How can we pray for you?

Pray for each person as a group.

Follow (Never skip)

Ask each person:
- How did you do with your commitments from last time?

Fish (Never skip)

Ask each person:
- Who did you share God's story/your story with?

Vision (Never skip)

Continue to encourage and give vision for winning souls by asking one of the following questions:
- What do you think God wants to do in your neighborhood/village?
- What do you want God to do in your family?
- What would it be like if the people in your neighborhood/village turned to God?

Look Up (1/3 of time)

Bible Study

Select a short story or passage from the Bible (e.g. Luke 10:1-5). Have each of the participants read the passage one verse at a time. Take a few moments to quietly reflect on the passage. Use the SOAP method or the three crosses method below.

Lead a discussion by asking the following questions:
- Which verse do you like best?
- Which verse is not clear to you or needs explanation?

The Center Cross

This represents Jesus, dying on the cross for us. Ask:
- What does this Scripture teach you about God?
- What do you see in this Scripture that reminds you of yourself?

The Left Cross

This represents the criminal who rejected and mocked Jesus. Ask:
- Is there an example in this Scripture that you should avoid?

The Right Cross

This represents the criminal who repented and Jesus promised him paradise. Ask:
- Is there an example in this Scripture that you want to follow?
- Is there a promise for you in this Scripture?

Look Forward (1/3 of time)

Follow and Fish (Never skip)

The facilitator should give the group time to ask the Holy Spirit to tell them how to live out the following questions.
- What do these verses teach you that you need to follow?
- Who will you share this passage, your story, or God's story with this week?

Wait at least one minute and then have the group write down and share their commitments.

Practice (Never skip)

If possible, practice your commitment with the group. If your commitment is to share the Gospel with a friend, practice telling your story or God's story with the group.

Commissioning Prayer

Have each person pray for one another for the courage to follow the Word and for His power to confirm the Word.

Note: This Bible Study format was adapted from Church Multiplication Coalition's (CMC) adaption of the Three-Thirds Process (Look Back, Look Up, Look Forward). More information about the Three-Thirds Process can be obtained from T4T Global Missions and E3 Partners. For more information you can also go to NoPlaceLeft.org. This page can be duplicated if done so in its entirety.

Treasure Hunts

Scripture

And He said to them, "Behold, when you have entered the city, a man will meet you carrying a pitcher of water; follow him into the house which he enters." - Luke 22:10

The woman answered and said, "I have no husband." Jesus said to her, "You have correctly said, 'I have no husband'; for you have had five husbands, and the one whom you now have is not your husband;" - John 4:17-18

Description

Treasure hunts, developed by Pastor Kevin Dedmon, are a way of doing outreach by using the gift of a word of knowledge. A word of knowledge (1 Cor. 12:8) is simply supernaturally knowing something that you would have no way of knowing otherwise. It can come to you as a thought, dream, impression, physical sensation, something you see or hear, or through any number of ways. You can ask the Lord for words of knowledge as clues to who He wants you to share the Gospel with.

Activation

- Get a blank piece of paper and write down the following categories with four or five spaces in each category. In a moment, you will fill in each space with clues for who the Lord wants you to find. Here are some **categories** to start with, but you could add your own as well: **Location / Appearance / Name / Prayer Need / Misc.**
- Ask Holy Spirit for what words to fill in for each space. You may have a picture of a person come to mind, a name pop into your head, remember a nearby place, or you may even just feel like you are making this up. However you receive your information, fill in ALL of your spaces in ALL of your categories.
- You can do this by yourself or in a group. If you are in a group, compare your lists with one another. Whether by yourself or in a group, pick a location to start and go there first (this works best if the location is nearby).
- Once you arrive at your location, start looking for the rest of the clues on your list.
- Take the list out with you, and when you find people that match your clues, show your list to them. Say, "We're on a treasure hunt and you're on our list. We asked God to show us people He wanted to bless and encourage and He led us to you. You are God's special treasure!"
- You can also show your list to people even if they don't seem to be on it and ask them if they match up with anything on your list.
- Ask them if you can pray for them. Feel free to prophesy over them as well and heal them if they are sick.
- Ask them if they know Jesus. If not, share the Gospel and lead them to Jesus.

Application

Using words of knowledge is a fun way to find people to minister to and is a great way to open up conversations with strangers. This method also works well to do with teenagers and children. Use and freely copy the treasure hunt list on the next page (used by permission).

Resource

Lesson taken from the book *Ultimate Treasure Hunt* by Kevin Dedmon, KevinDedmon.com

TREASURE HUNT

1. Each person writes down words of knowledge in the spaces allowed for each category:

   LOCATION (stop sign, store, bench, house, etc.)

   _____   _____   _____   _____   _____

   A PERSON'S NAME

   _____   _____   _____   _____   _____

   A PERSON'S APPEARANCE (color, clothing, hair, etc.)

   _____   _____   _____   _____   _____

   WHAT THEY NEED PRAYER FOR (knee, back brace, tumor, ears, etc.)

   _____   _____   _____   _____   _____

   THE UNUSUAL (Lollypop, dolphins, neon green pinwheel, etc.)

   _____   _____   _____   _____   _____

2. Get together in your group, compare your clues and decide where you will go.

3. Choose a beginning location.

4. Start finding out who you need to go to and begin talking to them.

5. When you find something on your list, let the Holy Spirit journey begin!
   Approach the person and say something like:
   "This may seem a little odd, but we're on a treasure hunt, and we think you're on our list."
   - SHOW THEM YOUR LIST. (Fold your sheet in half so you only show them the top half.)
   - Build rapport. (Make friends by asking questions about them to get to know them.)
   - Give them a prophetic word and bless them.
   - Ask if you can pray for them, then pray for them for healing or for other things.

6. If they say "no:"
   - Build more rapport (common ground - friendship).
   - Ask the Holy Spirit what He wants to highlight about the person.
   - Give them some encouraging and/or prophetic words.

7. Ask again if you can pray for them:
   - If they say "no" again, bless them and go to the next person!
   - If they say, "yes," ask for God's presence to come.
   - If it's for healing, command the pain to leave, life to come, etc. Then ask them to test it out by saying, "Do something you couldn't do before we prayed."

8. When they are healed and/or experience God's presence:
   - Explain what happened.
   - Ask them if they would like to know Jesus, personally.
   - Have them ask Jesus into their life!

9. Go to the next appointment. Write down the testimonies.

* This page can be duplicated if done so in its entirety.
* For more information see the book, *Ultimate Treasure Hunt*, by Kevin Dedmon, KevinDedmon.com.

Relational Outreach

Scripture
Behold, I stand at the door and knock. If anyone hears My voice and opens the door, I will come in to him and dine with him, and he with Me. - Revelation 3:20

Now it came to pass, as He sat at the table with them, that He took bread, blessed and broke it, and gave it to them. Then their eyes were opened and they knew Him; and He vanished from their sight. - Luke 24: 30-31

For I received from the Lord that which I also delivered to you: that the Lord Jesus on the same night in which He was betrayed took bread; and when He had given thanks, He broke it and said, "Take, eat; this is My body which is broken for you; do this in remembrance of Me." In the same manner He also took the cup after supper, saying, "This cup is the new covenant in My blood. This do, as often as you drink it, in remembrance of Me."
- 1 Corinthians 11:23-25

Description
When we open our hearts to Him, the Lord promises to come into our lives and eat with us. When Jesus broke bread and drank wine with His disciples, He said that they were to do these things in memory of Him—and then He would be in their midst. The disciples on the road to Emmaus didn't recognize Jesus until He broke bread. Whether we are in a formal communion service or simply eating together, we can honor the Lord in our hearts by intentionally setting aside meal times to be aware of His presence and invite unbelievers to join us. We can engage the Lord's presence and also connect with other people in either a more structured or more organic way. (Also see the lesson on Prayer Evangelism in the Transformation section on page 121 for an additional way of doing relational outreach.)

Activation 1 - Structured Model
Meet as a formal Christian group.
(See a model for setting up a small group in the Facilitator's Guide.)
- Host monthly, biweekly, or weekly Christian gatherings. When you meet, do the following:
  - Fellowship and connect with one another.
  - Break bread in communion and/or a shared meal.
  - Share testimonies of what Jesus is doing in your life.
  - Get in groups of two to three and minister (pray/prophesy) to each one's personal needs.
  - Have an optional time of worship and/or a Bible study/devotional/activation time.

Activation 2 - Organic Model
Have the same heart as in the model above, but with a less overt Christian structure.
- Have a meal with your friends and/or family and invite non-believers to attend.
- Pray together out loud before you eat and set the meal time apart for the Lord.
- Connect with the Lord and worship Him privately in your own heart during the time.
- Intentionally love those around you. Listen to them and ask questions to draw them out.
- Be yourself without an agenda and trust the Lord to lead your conversations.
- When or if it fits naturally in your conversations, share testimonies, prophesy over your guests and/or offer to pray for any needs they have already shared with you.

Application
As we invite others into our intentional eating and communing moments with the Lord, regardless of the setting, people will be affected by Jesus, and will draw closer to Him.

Spiritual Gifts

Now concerning spiritual gifts, brethren, I do not want you to be ignorant: There are diversities of gifts, but the same Spirit. There are differences of ministries, but the same Lord. And there are diversities of activities, but it is the same God who works all in all. But the manifestation of the Spirit is given to each one for the profit of all: for to one is given the word of wisdom through the Spirit, to another the word of knowledge through the same Spirit, to another faith by the same Spirit, to another gifts of healings by the same Spirit, to another the working of miracles, to another prophecy, to another discerning of spirits, to another different kinds of tongues, to another the interpretation of tongues. But one and the same Spirit works all these things, distributing to each one individually as He wills.
- 1 Corinthians 12:1,4-11

Pursue love, and desire spiritual gifts. . . . Even so you, since you are zealous for spiritual gifts, let it be for the edification of the church that you seek to excel. - 1 Corinthians 14:1a,12

For the gifts and the calling of God are irrevocable. - Romans 11:29

God gives us gifts for the benefit of others and not to draw attention to ourselves. Spiritual gifts are NOT a sign of our maturity, integrity, relationship with God, or even a guarantee that we are using them correctly. Spiritual gifts are powerful and we must learn to operate them for the benefit of others. (E.g. A car is a good thing but it could be used to help or harm people, depending on how it is used.) It is important that we operate in the gifts from the perspective of God's goodness and healthy mindsets of the kingdom.

We can, by faith, operate in any of the gifts at any time, depending on the need of the situation. All the gifts are available to all believers. If you prophesy, that does not make you a prophet any more than evangelizing makes you an evangelist. **Holy Spirit is the real gift, and He manifests Himself in different ways.**

We should rejoice that we know Jesus and are in relationship with Him. From that place of identity, we can rightly and powerfully use the gifts of the Holy Spirit to benefit others.

In this section and some of the sections to follow, we will briefly review some of the gifts of the Spirit listed in 1 Corinthians 12.

Holy Spirit Baptism

Scripture
And being assembled together with them, He commanded them not to depart from Jerusalem, but to wait for the Promise of the Father, "which," He said, "you have heard from Me; for John truly baptized with water, but you shall be baptized with the Holy Spirit not many days from now." - Acts 1:4-5

"But you shall receive power when the Holy Spirit has come upon you; and you shall be witnesses to Me in Jerusalem, and in all Judea and Samaria, and to the end of the earth." - Acts 1:8

And they were all filled with the Holy Spirit and began to speak with other tongues, as the Spirit gave them utterance. - Acts 2:4

And it shall come to pass in the last days, says God, that I will pour out of My Spirit on all flesh; your sons and your daughters shall prophesy, your young men shall see visions, your old men shall dream dreams. - Acts 2:17

And when they had prayed, the place where they were assembled together was shaken; and they were all filled with the Holy Spirit, and they spoke the word of God with boldness. - Acts 4:31

Description
At salvation, the Holy Spirit comes **inside** of us. Jesus told His followers who were already saved to wait to receive the baptism of the Holy Spirit before they went out into all the world. The baptism of the Spirit is when Holy Spirit comes **upon** us for power. In the Old Testament, leaders would pour oil on the heads of kings or priests to anoint them to lead. In the New Testament, Holy Spirit is poured out on all believers. Receiving the baptism of the Spirit enables us to walk in greater power and authority for ministry. In Scripture, believers who were filled with the Spirit often, but not always, spoke in other tongues, prophesied, and demonstrated other gifts of the Spirit. If you do not speak in tongues it does not mean that you did not receive the baptism of the Holy Spirit. People can be baptized or filled with the Holy Spirit once and then be continually filled again and again. Being filled with Holy Spirit is to be an ongoing process in our lives.

Activations
- Whether you have been baptized by the Holy Spirit before or not, ask God to fill you with His Holy Spirit and baptize you afresh.
- Have someone who already has the Holy Spirit baptism lay their hands on and pray for you.
- If you have already been baptized in the Holy Spirit, lay your hands on and pray for someone else to be baptized.
- While people do not always speak in tongues, many times they do. By faith, begin to speak in the Spirit and see what happens.

Application
Seek to be continually filled and refilled with Holy Spirit on a regular basis and pray for others to have this as well.

Tongues

Scripture
And these signs will follow those who believe: In My name they will cast out demons; they will speak with new tongues; - Mark 16:17

Cretans and Arabs—we hear them speaking in our own tongues the wonderful works of God. - Acts 2:11

And when Paul had laid hands on them, the Holy Spirit came upon them, and they spoke with tongues and prophesied. - Acts 19:6

. . . to another the working of miracles, to another prophecy, to another discerning of spirits, to another different kinds of tongues, to another the interpretation of tongues.
- 1 Corinthians 12:10

For he who speaks in a tongue does not speak to men but to God, for no one understands him; however, in the spirit he speaks mysteries. I wish you all spoke with tongues, but even more that you prophesied; for he who prophesies is greater than he who speaks with tongues, unless indeed he interprets, that the church may receive edification. But if there is no interpreter, let him keep silent in church, and let him speak to himself and to God.
- 1 Corinthians 14:2,5,28

Description
The gift of tongues is the ability to speak a language that we do not naturally know. We can speak with the tongues of men (natural languages, like on the day of Pentecost) or of angels (heavenly languages). Many people have been supernaturally given an earthly language to speak and even write without studying. You can receive tongues by asking God directly and/or having others who have the gift lay hands on you, and then begin to speak by faith. Sometimes people feel something when they speak in tongues and sometimes they do not.

If there is someone to interpret, tongues can at times be used to give a message to a group of believers. Tongues can also be used as a prayer language between us and the Lord. Even if there isn't anyone to interpret, it is okay to speak in tongues to yourself. You can even speak in tongues in a group, as long as it is in order with what is going on around you (e.g. a prayer meeting where everyone is praying out loud at the same time). You could even ask for the gift of tongues to speak the "language" of different areas of society like coding for software developers, different forms of math, engineering, etc. Like all gifts, tongues should be used in a way that edifies and builds people up in love, and it is no more or less important than any of the other gifts.

Activations
- If you don't yet pray in tongues, pray and ask to be able to. Now by faith start moving your mouth and speaking out loud.
- If you already speak in tongues, pray that you could interpret and/or ask for a new language. Now by faith pray in tongues and ask the Lord for the interpretation.
- Ask the Lord to give you an earthly language. By faith start speaking and see if you know what language you are speaking in.
- Ask for tongues for a language of society and begin to write and/or speak.

Application
Desire to speak in tongues and be open to the different ways that this gift can be powerfully received and used.

Word of Knowledge

Scripture
The woman answered and said, "I have no husband." Jesus said to her, "You have well said, 'I have no husband,' for you have had five husbands, and the one whom you now have is not your husband; in that you spoke truly." - John 4:17-18

And He said to them, "Behold, when you have entered the city, a man will meet you carrying a pitcher of water; follow him into the house which he enters." - Luke 22:10

Description
A word of knowledge is simply knowing something supernaturally that you would have no way of knowing otherwise. It helps a person to feel seen and known and builds their faith that God wants to lovingly encounter them. It can come to you as a thought, impression, memory, physical sensation (e.g. feeling pain in your body somewhere where you did not have pain before), something you see, hear, smell, taste, "see" in your mind, or through any number of ways. You can receive words of knowledge about the past, present, and the future.

For example, maybe you ask the Lord when a person was born and you see a picture of spring flowers. Then you ask the person if they were born in the spring. When they say, "Yes," ask the Lord what month it was. Or maybe you feel pain in your right knee and as you ask the Lord what that is about, you get the impression of a motorcycle and the number six. If you are in a group you could ask if anyone has pain in their right knee from a motorcycle accident six months or six years ago. If you feel like you have a word of knowledge it is good to ask an individual or a group if that is true of someone instead of stating something as fact. Since we are all learning this gives us room to be wrong if we didn't get the word completely right. Sometimes we get words of knowledge for people that are not even present but someone who is present knows them. If this happens someone could call or text them.

Activation
- Get a partner and ask the Lord for words of knowledge for them in the following areas:
  - Their favorite color.
  - Their middle name.
  - The month they were born (and date too, if you want to get specific).
  - Something they need physical healing for.

Application
When we share an accurate word of knowledge it gets people's attention. If we receive a word of knowledge for healing it is because the Lord is going to heal that area. Regularly ask the Lord to give you words of knowledge and then ask people questions to see if you are right. You can even practice with friends. If you ever feel like you get a word of knowledge about something negative in a person's life, instead of instantly sharing it, pray and ask the Lord what you are to do with the information (e.g. intercede, prophesy the solution, etc.). It can also be good to find a trusted leader to submit the word to who can help discern what is beneficial or appropriate to share or not and in what context. When you get a word of knowledge right, continue to follow the leading of the Lord for how He wants you to engage with that person. You can ask the Lord to give you a prophetic word to share with them, release healing, and see if they know Jesus.

Resource
Words of Knowledge by Randy Clark

Discerning of Spirits

Scripture
. . . to another the working of miracles, to another prophecy, to another discerning of spirits, to another different kinds of tongues, to another the interpretation of tongues.
- 1 Corinthians 12:10

Description
Discernment means to judge or know the difference between one thing and another. Discerning of spirits could be judging between God's Spirit and our spirit, what's going on in other people's spirits, or the happenings/presence of the spirits of angels and demons.

The devil is a liar and the father of lies. *"When he speaks a lie, he speaks from his own resources, for he is a liar and the father of it"* (John 8:44b). We do not need to ask him or his demons for help to discern spirits. The Holy Spirit of God inside of us is all we need. We do not go out of our way to look to see what the devil is doing. He is a defeated foe and what matters most is to see what God is doing.

If we discern something good we can call it out and agree with it. If we discern something negative we don't need to agree with what the enemy is doing. We should look to see what the solution to it is (i.e. ask what is true in heaven), and because our words have power, declare that out loud. Part of discernment is knowing what we are sensing that is ours and what we are sensing that is happening around us. We also seek the Lord for wisdom for when it is our place to simply observe something and when it is our place to do something about what we are discerning. The Lord will help us with this as we practice.

Activation
- Spend time, by yourself, soaking in the Lord's presence and being filled with His heart of love for you.
- Now walk into another room or group of people and see what feelings, thoughts, images, etc. come to you.
- If you sense something good, agree with it and bless it.
- We don't look for the negative, but if you discern something negative, declare what is true in heaven or a solution. For example, if you sense brokenness declare healing and wholeness, if you sense sadness release joy, if you sense anger or confusion release peace, etc. Speak this out loud, even if it is just a very quiet whisper.
- Ask the Lord to help you discern what may be going on around you and what He wants you, if anything, to do about it.

Application
Regularly ask the Lord to help you discern if what you are sensing is from heaven's perspective, within you, or from the atmosphere around you. When you discern what is happening around you ask the Lord how to partner with Him to release His kingdom.

Resource
Shifting Atmospheres by Dawna De Silva

Word of Wisdom

Scripture
. . . for to one is given the word of wisdom through the Spirit, to another the word of knowledge through the same Spirit. - 1 Corinthians 12:8

For the Lord gives wisdom; from His mouth come knowledge and understanding. - Proverbs 2:6

Then I (wisdom) was beside Him as a master craftsman; and I was daily His delight, rejoicing always before Him. - Proverbs 8:30

If any of you lacks wisdom, let him ask of God, who gives to all liberally and without reproach, and it will be given to him. But let him ask in faith, with no doubting, for he who doubts is like a wave of the sea driven and tossed by the wind. - James 1:5-6

Description
Wisdom is knowing what to do. It is not just looking at the options and knowing the difference between one or the other, or even the ability to pick the best of a group of options. Wisdom actually creates a new option that was not there before. When Peter went fishing and caught nothing all night Jesus told him to cast one more time on the other side of the boat (John 21:6). When the Jesus and Peter needed money to pay their taxes Jesus told Peter to go fishing and that the first fish he caught would have a coin in its mouth (Matthew 17:27). Sometimes the wisdom the Lord gives us will not make sense to us or it may seem very small and insignificant. It is important that when we pray for wisdom, we take immediate action on whatever the Lord leads us to do whether it makes sense to us or not.

Activation 1
- Pick an area of your life where you need wisdom and ask God, in faith, to show you what to do.
- Be open to the variety of ways that the Lord will reveal wisdom to you (His Word, another person, a dream, an inner knowing, etc.).
- Write down what the Lord revealed to you and go do it or take an action towards it.

Activation 2
- Pray together with a partner for a word of wisdom.
- Listen for the Lord to speak to you about your situation and also share if either of you sense anything for the other person.

Activation 3
- Read the chapter of Proverbs each day that matches the date on the calendar.
- As you read, ask the Lord for a word of wisdom for your day.
- At least three times a week, pick one proverb and rewrite it in your own words.
- If you miss a day, just move on to the current day without needing to catch up.

Application
When you come upon difficult situations, draw upon the word of wisdom gift to access creative solutions for yourself and others.

Physical Healing

Then Jesus went about all the cities and villages, teaching in their synagogues, preaching the gospel of the kingdom, and healing every sickness and every disease among the people. - Matthew 9:35

Most assuredly, I say to you, he who believes in Me, the works that I do he will do also; and greater works than these he will do, because I go to My Father. - John 14:12

But He was wounded for our transgressions, He was bruised for our iniquities; The chastisement for our peace was upon Him, And by His stripes we are healed. - Isaiah 53:5

Jesus healed every person who came to Him and He told us to do what He did. God's kingdom is perfect with no sickness or illness of any kind. God can't give sickness because He doesn't have any. Jesus told us to pray that God's kingdom would come on earth as it is in heaven, therefore it is our job to release healing in every form into the earth.

The most important thing we can do is follow the leading of the Holy Spirit, so we start by inviting Holy Spirit to come and touch the person to whom we are ministering. If we want to place a hand on them we ask them first and only touch them in appropriate places. We always pray with great compassion and care (Matt. 14:14) and keep our eyes open to see what God is doing. We should not get introspective to see if we feel holy enough or have read our Bible enough for God to use us. We know that all healing is very easy for Jesus and we should stay more focused on Him than on ourselves or the problem.

When Jesus or the disciples ministered healing they spoke out loud and/or took some kind of action. Therefore, when we heal the sick we speak words of faith and healing out loud rather than simply thinking them. Just like James 2:17 says that faith without works is dead, we have people put their faith in action and immediately test out their healing to see what God is doing. If they are not yet completely healed we can declare healing for them again like Jesus did in Mark 8:25. We declare with great authority just like we would boldly command a big angry dog to get away from approaching a small child. We command out loud for all pain and sickness to leave and say, "Be healed. Pain get out in Jesus' name." We always pray with faith for instant healing (Matt. 9:29), but know that even if we don't see an immediate change, some healing comes over time (Luke 17:14). Jesus didn't heal the same way twice, so healing the sick is more about being connected to His heart than a method. In this section we will look at some basic principles for ministering healing.

Resources
Power to Heal and *School of Healing and Impartation* by Randy Clark - GlobalAwakening.com, *Unlocking Heaven* by Kevin Dedmon, *Walking in Supernatural Healing Power* by Chris Gore, PaulRapley.com

Five Step Healing Model

Scripture
Heal the sick, cleanse the lepers, raise the dead, cast out demons. Freely you have received, freely give. - Matthew 10:8

Description
This is a powerful model for healing. You can remember each step by looking at the fingers on your hand. Even as we learn healing models, remember we always focus on the Prince (Jesus) more than the principles.

Activation

1. **Interview:** Find a partner and ask them, "Do you have any pain in your body or anything that keeps your body from working perfectly?" Have them tell you in 30 seconds or less. If it is something they feel right now, have them give you a number of how bad it hurts on a scale of 1-10 (with 1 being hardly any pain and 10 being excruciating pain). Ask, "Can I put my hand on you?" Do so if it is a place that is appropriate to put a hand. Otherwise, have the person put their hand where they need healing and put your hand on top of their hand or on their shoulder. Keep your eyes open to see what is happening.

2. **Declare**: Invite the Lord to touch them by saying, "Holy Spirit, come." Turn your heart toward them in love and compassion and rest in the presence of the Lord. Declare out loud with authority, "Pain, go in Jesus' name." "(<u>Name their specific conditions</u>) be healed now in Jesus' name." If needed, encourage the person to simply receive and not to pray with you. You don't need to pray for a long time.

3. **Test**: Have the person test it out or do something they couldn't do before to put their faith in action. Ask what number the pain is at now. See if they feel any better or not.

4. **Repeat if Needed:** If it's 100% healed then celebrate! If they sense some percentage of healing, give thanks for what has happened and declare healing again. If they feel no change, encourage them and declare healing over them again.

5. **Follow Up:** Encourage the person with how much Jesus loves them and to give thanks for whatever level of healing they received. If they weren't fully healed it is NOT your job to figure out why (DON'T wonder if they or you had enough faith or not). Remind them that every time we pray something happens, some healings happen over time, and that they should continue seeking the Lord for full healing. If they don't know Jesus, lead them to the Lord. If you are in a group, have people who were healed raise their hands, holding up a finger for each condition they were healed of. Count them and share testimonies.

Application
Use this model with people both inside and outside of church and to teach others to heal.

* The original version of this model was developed by John Wimber of the Vineyard Church.

Words of Knowledge for Healing

Scripture
For to one is given the word of wisdom through the Spirit, and to another the word of knowledge according to the same Spirit. - 1 Corinthians 12:8

Description
A word of knowledge is knowing something supernaturally that you would have no way of knowing otherwise. It can come to you as a thought, impression, physical sensation, something you see or hear, or through any number of ways. When we get a word of knowledge for healing it is to release faith to that person that God is going to heal them.

For example, if your arm begins to hurt but it didn't hurt a few minutes ago, ask the people around you if any of them have anything wrong with their arm. Or if you see a mental picture of someone falling off a bicycle, ask those around you if any of them were ever injured in a bike accident.

Activation 1
- Pair up with someone and ask the Lord to give you words of knowledge for what they need healing for. Try to be as specific as possible.
- Share the words you have for them until you get three wrong, and then switch partners.
- Declare healing over each other.

Activation 2
- Write down a list of words of knowledge for healing and who they are for. For example you may write down, "Woman in a yellow sweater with right shoulder pain."
- Keep the list with you and look for the people on it as you go throughout your day.
- As you find them, approach them and ask if they have those physical ailments. If they do you can show them your list to build their faith.
- Minister healing to them and see if they know Jesus.

Application
Be sensitive to when the Lord is giving you words of knowledge for others. Release what you are sensing by asking questions to see if they are right. Have confidence that the Lord is going to touch the person for whom you had the word of knowledge. Also know that sometimes you may have words of knowledge for people that aren't in the room when the words are released. You, or others in the meeting, may find these people at a later time.

Resource
Words of Knowledge by Randy Clark

Additional Healing Activations

Scripture
And heal the sick there, and say to them, "The kingdom of God has come near to you."
- Luke 10:9

Description
These are additional powerful ways to activate people in healing. Since you are teaching people a potentially new model of healing, tell them to please wait to pray until you tell them what to do, step by step, at least one or two times. Encourage people to honestly share ALL their healing needs. To build people's faith, share healing testimonies or videos or demonstrate the activation for the group before activating them. Have those who were healed raise their hands high, holding up a finger for each condition they were healed of and count them. Have some people share briefly the major things they were healed of and even have people who need a breakthrough in that area go to them for prayer.

Activation 1 - Large Group Healing
- Give words of knowledge for people with specific conditions, or ask anyone who needs a healing of any kind to stand up and raise their hand high in the air.
- Have everyone who is sitting stand up and go to a person with their hand raised. Tell those with their hands raised to put their hands down when someone has come to them.
- Make sure everyone who needs prayer has someone praying for them.
- Walk them through the five step prayer model.

Activation 2 - Holy Spirit and Compassion
- Use the activation exercise "Feeling God's Presence" in the Outreach section to have people practice inviting the Lord to touch their partner. As they do this encourage them to focus on having compassion for their partner. Interview people to see what they experienced and have them check their bodies to see if some of them are already healed.

Activation 3 - Legs Grow Out
- In groups of two have one person at a time sit far back in a chair and put their legs straight out in front of them. Have their partner look at the heels of their shoes to see if one leg is shorter than the other. If it is, command the shorter leg to grow in Jesus' name.

Activation 4 - Groups of 3
This is a powerful way for people to minister healing multiple times. (Created by Paul Rapley.)
- Have people get into groups of 3 with people that they do not know well.
- Tell them to designate which person is person 1, person 2, and person 3.
- Have person 3 go first and tell the others in 20 seconds or less what they need healing for.
- Have person 1 and 2 take 60 seconds and repeat after you saying, "Pain go in Jesus' name. (Specific issues) be healed in Jesus' name!" Now do the same for person 2.
- For person 3 have the other two practice sharing words of knowledge for healing (see the previous page). Person 3 can say if the words were right or not and then share any other healing needs. Let person 1 and 2 pray for person 3 on their own (without you leading them).
- Have everyone in the group test out how they are feeling and see who is healed.
- If anyone needs more healing, give them 60 seconds per person to pray for each person in the group again.

Prophecy

My sheep hear My voice, and I know them, and they follow Me. - John 10:27

Pursue love, and desire spiritual gifts, but especially that you may prophesy . . . . But the one who prophesies speaks to people for their strengthening, encouraging and comfort.
- 1 Corinthians 14:1,3

Our Father is a really good Dad who dearly loves His kids! Like any good father, He loves interacting with us by talking to us, leading us, and showing us things. He made us and knows the best way to communicate with us. Unlike some of the Old Testament where only anointed people could hear from God or prophesy, in the New Testament all believers have the Holy Spirit and can both hear from God for themselves and prophesy over others. Jesus said that we are His sheep, and because of that, we hear His voice. New Testament prophecy is for edification, exhortation, and comfort. Another way to say this is to build up, stir up, or cheer up.

When we prophesy, we only listen to hear or look to see the good things that are true in heaven. If we sense something negative we don't say it but rather flip it to make it into a positive. We do not always need to share everything we sense for a person but can filter what we are receiving and share whatever is most beneficial for that person to hear. We use language such as, "I feel like God is saying," when sharing prophetic words so that the person receiving the word has room to judge the word for themselves. We do not prophesy directional words such as dates, mates, or babies. Just because someone says, "God told me," does not necessarily mean that God told them. We each get to be powerful and decide if we will fully or partially receive the words others give us or if we will flush those words as not being from God.

All believers hear from God and the Lord speaks to us in a variety of ways. Many times He speaks to us by giving us impressions or images (pictures) in our mind. Just like there are songs and images in any given room at one time, and those with a radio or internet on a cell phone can tune into them, so we can choose to tune into the good things that God is saying. The heart of all prophecy is to communicate love and to point people to the reality of what is true in heaven over their lives. Just like treasure hunters, we do not need to talk about the dirt that we see in people's lives, rather we call out the gold that we find and draw attention to what is good, true, and precious inside of them.

In this section we will look at some basic principles for hearing God's good voice for ourselves and how to prophetically minister good things to others. For a more in depth explanation and an interactive skit on prophecy from the Old to New Testament, see the pages at the end of this section.

Resources
Prophetic trainings, books, and teachings by Dan McCollam - PropheticCompany.com, Kris Vallotton - KrisVallotton.com, and Shawn Bolz - BolzMinistries.com.

Ways God Speaks

Here is a list of some of the ways that the Lord communicates with His kids. Sometimes the Lord speaks very clearly and directly. Other times what God says needs interpretation to understand what it means, who it is for, how it should be applied, and when it may happen. As we stay in connection to the Lord and His body of believers, we will grow in learning how to hear, understand, and apply what He tells us.

Audible and Inner Voice - John 10:27

Still Small Voice - 1 Kings 19:11-13

The Bible - 2 Peter 1:20

Nature - Romans 1:20a

Visions - Genesis 15:1

Night Visions - Job 33:13-16

Dreams - Matthew 2:12

Parables - Matthew 13:34-35

Dark Sayings - Psalm 78:2

Words of Knowledge - 1 Corinthians 12:8

Words of Wisdom - 1 Corinthians 12:8

Songs - 1 Corinthians 14:15

Tongues - 1 Corinthians 14:13

Face to Face - Numbers 12:6-8a

Other Believers - Proverbs 15:22 and 1 Corinthians 14:31-32

Activation
- Write down and share with a partner the different ways that God speaks to you.

Strengthen, Encourage, and Comfort

Scripture
But the one who prophesies speaks to people for their strengthening, encouraging and comfort. - 1 Corinthians 14:3 (NIV)

Description
Prophecy is something that strengthens, encourages, or comforts. Another way to say this is that it builds people up, stirs them up, and cheers them up. Prophecy is the good things that God, as a good dad, wants to speak to us as His good kids. Prophecy causes us to draw near to God and adds momentum to our lives.

Activation 1
Pair up with another person and do each of the following:
- Offer a compliment and say something good about them (e.g. "You have a nice smile.").
- Say something encouraging about them or give a generally encouraging word.
- Find out if they need comfort in any area of their life, and demonstrate comfort to them.

Activation 2
- Stay with your same partner.
- Say the exact same things that you said in the last activation but now turn them into prophetic words. As you say each one again, pause and ask the Lord to show you more good things that He wants to share with them.
  - E.g. "You have a nice smile, and I feel like God is saying that He is going to use you to bring joy to a lot of people."

Application
Oftentimes we just need to start speaking or thinking good things about a person. Out of that the Lord will show us more good things about them and give us prophetic words to share with them.

* Lesson inspired by Pastor Jamey VanGelder, The House Church and Pastor David Olson, SkyWater Church

Name-Based Prophecies

Scripture
A good name is to be chosen rather than great riches. - Proverbs 22:1a

And I also say to you that you are Peter, and on this rock I will build My church, and the gates of Hades shall not prevail against it. - Matthew 16:18

No longer shall your name be called Abram, but your name shall be Abraham; for I have made you a father of many nations. - Genesis 17:5

Description
All throughout the Bible, the Lord talks to people about how their names are connected to their identity and destiny. Name-based prophetic words are fun and easy conversation starters that can lead to powerful God encounters. As you are in a conversation with someone, you can simply ask them a question about their name, or start sharing something that comes to mind for them about their name. As with all prophecy, you do NOT need to tell the person that you are prophesying over them. Simply start encouraging them and share the good things God puts on your heart in the midst of a conversation.

Activation 1 - How Awesome You Are
- Find someone and ask them, "Can I tell you how awesome you are, based on your name?"
- When they say, "Yes," do one of the following activations.

Activation 2 - First Letter
- Tell your partner a prophetic word based on the **first letter** of their first name.

Activation 3 - Each Letter
- Give them a prophetic word based on **each letter** of their first name.
- This can be something you speak out loud or write down for them.

Activation 4 - Name Meaning
- Find out a person's name, and then ask them, "Do you know what your name means?"
- Whether they know the meaning or not, give them a prophetic word either based on what they share or about how you feel the Lord wants to encourage them regarding their name.

Application
Name-based prophecies are fast, easy, and so encouraging to do with almost anyone. They are especially great to do with people who wear name tags or when you first meet someone. You can also prophecy over people who remind you of someone you know by saying, "You remind me of my friend _____." Then share what similarities you sense they have in common. Try doing one name prophecy a day for a week.

Image-Based Prophecies

Scripture
Again He said to me, "Prophesy to these bones, and say to them, 'O dry bones, hear the word of the Lord!'" - Ezekiel 37:4

So Moses made a bronze serpent, and put it on a pole; and so it was, if a serpent had bitten anyone, when he looked at the bronze serpent, he lived. - Numbers 21:9

Description
Like Ezekiel had a vision of dry bones that represented the nation of Israel, many times we will see an image or sense an impression for someone that means something else. Like the serpent on the pole, an image inspired by the Lord can bring healing and hope. We can see not only with our physical eyes, but also in our minds, or we could say in our imagination. This does not mean that we are simply imagining or making something up, but rather that when we submit our minds and imaginations to the Lord, He will use these places like a canvas or a movie screen to show us things He wants us to see. Like all forms of prophecy, it is okay if what we see doesn't make sense to us right away because we can ask the Lord what it is that He wants to communicate. Sometimes we see something and it is best to simply tell someone about it. Other times it is powerful to draw, find, or create an actual image to communicate this word to another person.

Activation 1
- Ask the Lord to show you a picture in your mind for your partner and ask Him what it means for them.
- Tell your partner, "This is the picture I believe I saw for you and this is what I feel like it means for you."

Activation 2
- Ask the Lord to give you a simple picture for your partner and then draw it for them. Even if you do not have a picture come to mind, you can simply start drawing and see what comes out. Try to keep the drawing very simple and when you share it, do not apologize for it being very simple.
- Tell your partner, "I drew this picture for you and this is what I feel like it means."
- You can also write a word or two on the picture if you would like.

Activation 3
- Ask the Lord to give you a literal picture for your partner like a photograph, a picture of something online, an image in a magazine, etc.
- Give or show your partner the photo, picture, or image and share what it means for them.

Application
Image-based prophecies are powerful and practical ways to encourage, strengthen, and comfort others. People love receiving either a picture you describe or an actual, physical image with a special meaning just for them.

It's All About Love

Scripture
And though I have the gift of prophecy, and understand all mysteries and all knowledge, and though I have all faith, so that I could remove mountains, but have not love, I am nothing. . . Love suffers long and is kind; love does not envy; love does not parade itself, is not puffed up; does not behave rudely, does not seek its own, is not provoked, thinks no evil; does not rejoice in iniquity, but rejoices in the truth; bears all things, believes all things, hopes all things, endures all things. Love never fails. But whether there are prophecies, they will fail; whether there are tongues, they will cease; whether there is knowledge, it will vanish away. For we know in part and we prophesy in part. But when that which is perfect has come, then that which is in part will be done away. - 1 Corinthians 13:2, 4-10

Description
First Corinthians chapter twelve talks about spiritual gifts, chapter thirteen talks about love, and chapter fourteen talks about prophecy. In the middle, and the most important part, is love! It is important that people experience the love of God when you prophesy over them. As you minister, be asking the Lord how He wants to demonstrate His love both through what is spoken and through how it is released.

Activation
- Look at your partner and ask the Lord to help you experience His love for them. Lean your heart towards them without even speaking.
- Now begin to speak or minister and release a prophetic word that helps them to experience God's love for them.
- Ask the Lord for a prophetic word and a way to release it that would really help your partner encounter His love.
- As you share the word, take time to pay attention to how the person you are ministering to is receiving. For example, if they start crying or encountering Holy Spirit strongly, then pause and let the Lord minister to them before you continue talking.

Application
No matter how precise or general our words are, what is really important is that we communicate the heart of love that Father God has for the person to whom we are ministering. If we can help someone to feel truly loved, we have succeeded!

Processing Prophecy

Scripture
Moreover the word of the Lord came to me, saying, "Jeremiah, what do you see?" And I said, "I see a branch of an almond tree." Then the Lord said to me, "You have seen well, for I am ready to perform My word." - Jeremiah 1:11-12

Description
Oftentimes we see or sense something from the Lord, but we don't immediately know what it means or what we should do with it. It is good for us to take time to ask the Lord a couple of questions so we will know what it means, how to best share it with others, and how we could apply it.

Revelation is what you see or sense. It is the information you feel like God is showing you.
Interpretation is what you believe the information means.
Communication is how best to share the information and meaning with another person.
Application is how the word will be applied to a person's life, and is ultimately up to them to decide how to take action.

Activation
- **Revelation**: Find a partner and ask the Lord for a prophetic word for them. You can ask Him something like, "Please show me something for my partner," or, "What do You want to say to my partner?" Maybe you see a picture of a teddy bear in your imagination.
- **Interpretation**: Now before you share what you received with your partner, ask the Lord, "What does what You showed me mean for my partner?" Maybe the teddy bear that He showed you means that He wants to bring comfort to them. Maybe it means they have permission to be like a child before Him. Or maybe an actual teddy bear means something to them and you won't have to say more.
- **Communication**: Ask the Lord, "What is the best way for me to share this?"
  - For example, you might share:
    - **Only what you saw or sensed**: "I see an image of a teddy bear. Does that mean anything to you?"
    - **What you saw or sensed and what you felt like it meant**: "I saw a picture of a teddy bear and feel like it means that God wants you to know you can be like a little child with Him."
    - **Only what it meant**: "I feel like God is wanting to give you good gifts that will comfort your heart."
- **Application**: The application of a word is up to the person receiving it to discern with the Lord and should never be told to them. When receiving a strong prophetic word it is wise to invite feedback from trusted people as to how to apply the word to your life.

Application
When receiving prophetic words for others, take time to ask the Lord questions about what the word means and how to share it. Then only share what is useful for the other person.

Rapid Fire Prophecy

Scripture
And as you go, preach, saying, "The kingdom of heaven is at hand." - Matthew 10:7

Then Philip opened his mouth, and beginning at this Scripture, preached Jesus to him. - Acts 8:35

Description
Oftentimes we just need the courage to go and to start. As we get started in prophecy, it becomes very easy to continue to hear from the Lord and keep going. We can start at any place and, by faith, choose to prophesy over someone.

Activation
- This works best in a group. Have people line up in two lines, facing each other, so that each person has someone standing directly across from them. Each person can shake hands with the person across from them to make sure everyone has only one partner. Tell them that one line will stay still the whole time and the other line will move one person to their right when it's time to change partners. The person on the very end of the moving line will have to go around to where that line started.

- Tell them: "I'm going to give you a category and then you will have 60 seconds (total or per person, depending on your preference) to prophesy over your partner using that category. After you both prophesy over each other, you will get a new partner and I'll give you a different category."

- Use the following categories or think of new ones:
    - Color
    - Shape
    - Something They are Wearing
    - Food
    - Song (Bonus if You Sing it)
    - Movie
    - Animal
    - One Word
    - Something in the Room
    - Prophetic Act
    - Number
    - Place
    - Texture
    - Season
    - Name
    - What Time it is Right Now

E.g. "You are like _____ because _____."
  - "You are like the season spring because you carry new life."
  - "You are like the color black because you understand God's mysteries."
  - "You are like a circle because the love that you have for others goes on forever."

Application
Be able to prophesy concisely, concretely, and quickly, starting from any place. Trust what the Lord gives you even when you don't have a lot of time to think about it.

Hearing from God, Prophecy, and the Holy Spirit in the Old and New Testament

This is a deeper look at how people have heard from God, interacted with the Holy Spirit, and prophesied between the Old and New Testament. When prophesying, it is important that we do so from a New Testament perspective. Many of us may have only seen a more Old Testament version of prophecy demonstrated. This looks like prophets who speak on behalf of God what are oftentimes harsh, negative, and directive prophetic words. The next few pages can help us to build a bridge from that understanding to a healthy, New Testament perspective.

In the very beginning, God's kids walked and talked with Him in the Garden of Eden. *"And they heard the sound of the Lord God walking in the garden in the cool of the day, and Adam and his wife hid themselves from the presence of the Lord God among the trees of the garden. Then the Lord God called to Adam and said to him, 'Where are you?'"* (Genesis 3:8-9).

When sin entered the world, people began to hide from God, although the Lord continued to talk to His children throughout the Old Testament. Over time, people began to ask for leaders to hear from God for them and help rule them. Moses wanted everyone to hear from the Lord themselves. *"Then Moses said to him, 'Are you zealous for my sake? Oh, that all the Lord's people were prophets and that the Lord would put His Spirit upon them!'"* (Numbers 11:29). Sadly, the children of Israel were too afraid to hear from God for themselves so they asked Moses to talk with God for them. *"Then they said to Moses, 'You speak with us, and we will hear; but let not God speak with us, lest we die'"* (Exodus 20:19). In 1 Samuel 8 the people demanded a king so they could be like other nations, even though the Lord wanted to be their king. This began a season of time where special people were anointed for special roles to hear from God, prophesy, and rule over others.

In the Old Testament, those who followed the Lord did not have the Holy Spirit inside of them because Jesus had not yet paid for our sins to restore us back to the Father. Only selected individuals, like prophets, priests, judges, or kings, had the Holy Spirit come upon them to give them power to perform their God ordained service. This is why leaders (like Elijah in 1 Kings 19:16) would pour out oil upon people to anoint them for service. This was a picture of Holy Spirit (the oil) coming upon that person in power to perform a certain role.

In the Old Testament, Holy Spirit empowered the prophets to speak on behalf of God, the priests to minister full time to the Lord, and the kings to rule the people. Because the average believer could not hear from God for themselves, prophets who spoke things that did not happen were to be put to death. *"But the prophet who presumes to speak a word in My name, which I have not commanded him to speak, or who speaks in the name of other gods, that prophet shall die"* (Deuteronomy 18:20).

However, all of this changed when Jesus came! Jesus told all of His followers that they could hear His voice and after He left, He said He would send the Holy Spirit to all of them to teach them. *"My sheep hear My voice, and I know them, and they follow Me"* (John 10:27).

> *"And I will pray the Father, and He will give you another Helper, that He may abide with you forever— the Spirit of truth, whom the world cannot receive, because it neither sees Him nor knows Him; but you know Him, for He dwells with you and will be in you. I will not leave you orphans; I will come to you."* - John 14:16-18

> *"But the Helper, the Holy Spirit, whom the Father will send in My name, He will teach you all things, and bring to your remembrance all things that I said to you"* - John 14:26

When Jesus rose from the dead He found His disciples and gave them the Holy Spirit to live inside of them. The word in this verse for "breathed on" literally means to "breathe into," like when God breathed into Adam the breath of life. [1]

> *"So Jesus said to them again, 'Peace to you! As the Father has sent Me, I also send you.' And when He had said this, He breathed on them, and said to them, 'Receive the Holy Spirit. . .'"* - John 20:21-22

After this, Jesus told His followers to wait for the Holy Spirit to come upon them in power.

> *And being assembled together with them, He commanded them not to depart from Jerusalem, but to wait for the Promise of the Father, "which," He said, "you have heard from Me; for John truly baptized with water, but you shall be baptized with the Holy Spirit not many days from now." Therefore, when they had come together, they asked Him, saying, "Lord, will You at this time restore the kingdom to Israel?" And He said to them, "It is not for you to know times or seasons which the Father has put in His own authority. But you shall receive power when the Holy Spirit has come upon you; and you shall be witnesses to Me in Jerusalem, and in all Judea and Samaria, and to the end of the earth."* - Acts 1:4-8.

Once Jesus had gone back into heaven, the Holy Spirit came in power on the day of Pentecost.

> *But this is what was spoken by the prophet Joel: "And it shall come to pass in the last days, says God, That I will pour out My Spirit on all flesh; Your sons and your daughters shall prophesy, Your young men shall see visions, Your old men shall dream dreams. And on My menservants and on My maidservants I will pour out My Spirit in those days; And they shall prophesy."* - Acts 2:16-18.

Now ALL believers in Jesus have access to both the Holy Spirit of God living on the inside of us and coming upon us in power in ways that only prophets, priests, judges, and kings had access to in the Old Testament.

Paul tells us about spiritual gifts in 1 Corinthians 12 and the importance of love in 1 Corinthians 13. Whatever gift manifests, it all comes from the same Holy Spirit. It must benefit everyone and also be done in love.

> *Now concerning spiritual gifts, brethren, I do not want you to be ignorant . . . But the manifestation of the Spirit is given to each one for the profit of all: for to one is given the word of wisdom through the Spirit, to another the word of knowledge through the same Spirit, to another faith by the same Spirit, to another gifts of healings by the same Spirit, to another the working of miracles, to another prophecy, to another discerning of spirits, to another different kinds of tongues, to another the interpretation of tongues.* - 1 Corinthians 12:1,7-10

> *And though I have the gift of prophecy, and understand all mysteries and all knowledge, and though I have all faith, so that I could remove mountains, but have not love, I am nothing.* - 1 Corinthians 13:2

We are to pursue love and desire that we can prophesy. *"Pursue love, and desire spiritual gifts, but especially that you may prophesy"* (1 Corinthians 14:1).

---

[1] Arthur W. Pink, Exposition of the Gospel of John, p. 1100 - BlueLetterBible.org

As we prophesy it will be to strengthen others, encourage them, and comfort them. *"But the one who prophesies speaks to people for their strengthening, encouraging and comfort"* (1 Corinthians 14:3).

All believers can now have the Holy Spirit inside of them, be baptized in His power, hear from God, and prophesy over others. Unlike in the Old Testament where leaders were there to hear from God for others, minister full time, or rule others, now leaders are supposed to equip believers to hear from God for themselves, prophesy, minister, and be able to rule their own lives. *"And He Himself gave some to be apostles, some prophets, some evangelists, and some pastors and teachers, for the equipping of the saints for the work of ministry, for the edifying of the body of Christ"* (Ephesians 4:11-12). Not everyone is called to be a prophet. This is not something we seek but if God calls us to this, other leaders in that office will confirm it and the fruit of our lives should be that we help others to hear from God for themselves and have healthy prophetic ministry.

Now that all of us as believers can have the Holy Spirit on the inside and outside of us, hear from God for ourselves, and prophesy, this also means that all believers can and should judge or discern the words that are shared with them. Paul says in 1 Corinthians 14:31-32 that everyone can prophesy one by one, that all may be encouraged and others can judge the words. Just because someone tells us that God is telling them something for us does not necessarily mean that is what God is saying to us. Since we can hear from God for ourselves, it is our responsibility to decide if that is what God is telling us or not. We do not have to receive every prophetic word that people share with us.

In 1 Kings 13:15-26 there is a strange story about a man who the Lord told to not eat until he got home. On his way home he met a prophet who invited him for a meal. The prophet lied to the man and told him an angel had appeared to him and said it was okay for the man to eat. The man believed the prophet above the word the Lord had given to him directly and actually died because of it. In Acts 21:10-14 the prophet Agabus gave Paul a prophetic word to try to convince him not to go to Jerusalem, but Paul said the Lord talked with him and told him that he needed to go.

In both of these stories we see that prophets and prophetic people can be wrong or simply not interpret a word correctly. Unlike in the Old Testament, we do not kill people if their words do not come to pass, but we do need to take responsibility to hear from God for ourselves, no matter what other people say God is telling them for us. We also learn from this that we should be responsible for the prophetic words that we give to others. Obviously we should never lie to someone like the man in 1 Kings did, but even if we get an interpretation of a word wrong, like Agabus, we should go to the person affected by our word and talk with them, apologizing if necessary.

We can test the effect of our prophetic ministry by looking at the root and the fruit. Are we rooted in hope and love or are we rooted solely in accuracy and "truth" apart from love? Truth must be spoken in love (Ephesians 4:15) such that the effect of any word is freedom, hope, and life for the person receiving ministry. If our prophetic ministry creates a sense of fear, judgement, hopelessness, dependency upon a prophet to hear from God, etc., then even if our information is "correct" we are out of line with the fruit of the Spirit which is *"love, joy, peace, longsuffering, kindness, goodness, faithfulness, gentleness, self-control . . ."* (Galatians 5:22-23).

Because New Testament prophecy is only to bring encouragement, strength, and comfort we only speak out what is true in heaven when giving words. We never speak prophetic words of death or judgement over people and we do not try to direct or control people's lives. Since all prophecy is rooted in heaven, that means it is rooted in hope and should always carry a sense of hope. Since Paul says we should pursue love as we desire spiritual gifts, all prophetic words should be rooted in love and communicate the love of God to the person receiving them.

A Skit About the Role of the Holy Spirit, Prophets, and Prophecy In the Old and New Testament

This skit gives a visual demonstration for how the role of the Holy Spirit, prophets, leaders, and prophecy were different in the Old Testament than they are for believers today. This can be very powerful to show people, especially if they are coming from a strong Old Testament background where prophecy is seen as judgmental or something that only anointed prophets can do. The goal of this skit is to bridge the gap between prophecy and hearing from God in the Old Testament verses today in order to help people understand why biblically we must have a different prophetic culture today. It also shows how leaders led differently in the Old Testament before all believers had access to the Holy Spirit for themselves.

Overview:
- Have a narrator read this script while volunteers silently act out different roles.
- Only the narrator (or anyone assisting them) should have a book, and not the actors.
- This works best if you can practice ahead of time. However, if you can't practice, you can simply call people up and help them act this out as you read through it. If doing this without a rehearsal you could have another person with a book helping give direction to the actors while the Narrator reads.
- It can be helpful for actors to wear a sign stating their role.
- It is okay if this skit is a little messy as long as the audience can still understand its meaning. People will enjoy participating and seeing people they know acting in the skit.
- If working with a younger audience, make sure to keep the skit moving.

The Narrator Will:
- Ask for eight volunteers and make sure at least three are female and at least three are male.
- Tell each person what role(s) they are playing after they come up front. The Prophet and Holy Spirit can be good roles to give to females. Note that five people will have two roles.
- Have the Godhead stand to the right of the narrator and the other five stand to the left.
- Instruct all actors to face center stage so that they have their sides turned to the audience, and form a "V" shape, with the narrowest point by the Narrator, so all actors can be clearly seen. Tell the actors that when they are called to step out they should do so at the widest part of the "V," closest to the audience so they can best be seen.
- Tell the actors they can face the audience or stand sideways but they should never have their backs turned to the audience.
- Tell the actors and audience who each person represents and that as they read about each role each actor will step forward to the middle, act out their part, and then step back in line with the others.
- Tell the actors that they can use their imaginations and be creative in how they each act out their roles.

Script Format:
Narrator: The narrator reads the words in bold to the audience.

Action: Actions for the actors are listed next, in regular font. These show directions for the narrator, or another person, to motion to the actors or read to them, quietly, if necessary.

Scripture: Bible verses are listed last in italics. These can be read or not, depending on your audience and how much time you have. The Narrator or another person could read these.

Roles:
- Average Believer/King
- Average Believer/Prophet
- Average Believer/Peter
- Average Believer/Paul
- Average Believer/Priest
- Father God
- Jesus
- Holy Spirit

SCRIPT

Narrator: "In the Old Testament, the Holy Spirit came upon and anointed special people to give them power to do certain tasks. He came upon Priests to minister to God and to care for people."

Action: Holy Spirit, the Priest, and Father God step forward. The Priest faces the Godhead and Holy Spirit acts out coming upon him. Facing Father God, the Priest acts out bowing low and ministering to God and continues acting this out until told to step back in line.

Scripture: *Aaron was set apart, he and his sons forever, that he should sanctify the most holy things, to burn incense before the Lord, to minister to Him, and to give the blessing in His name forever. - 1 Chronicles 23:13b*

Narrator: "Holy Spirit came upon Kings so they could rule the people."

Action: The King steps forward, standing in front of Holy Spirit, and facing the rest of the "average believers." Holy Spirit acts out coming upon the King and the King acts out ruling the people with the people obeying him. He keeps doing this until told to step back in line.

Scripture: *"Also you shall anoint Jehu the son of Nimshi as king over Israel. And Elisha the son of Shaphat of Abel Meholah you shall anoint as prophet in your place." - 1 Kings 19:16*

Narrator: "Holy Spirit also came upon Prophets to speak on behalf of God to the people."

Action: The Prophet steps forward. The Prophet faces the "average believers," standing in front of Father God and Holy Spirit. Holy Spirit acts out coming upon the Prophet. Father God cups His hands around His mouth and acts out speaking into the Prophet's ear. As He does, the Prophet moves his mouth and hands to show he is speaking on behalf of God. The other believers look as if they are listening and understanding what is being said.

Scripture: *"Surely the Lord God does nothing, unless He reveals His secret to His servants the prophets." - Amos 3:7*

"Neither have we heeded Your servants the prophets, who spoke in Your name to our kings and our princes, to our fathers and all the people of the land." - Daniel 9:6

Narrator: "In the New Testament, all of this changed!"

Action: All actors step back into their "V" line.

Narrator: "Jesus came to earth and gathered many followers. He said that all of His sheep hear His voice and follow Him."

Action: Jesus steps forward and begins to mouth words and move his hands to the average believers. The believers look like they are listening and are excited about what He is telling them.

Scripture: *"My sheep hear My voice, and I know them, and they follow Me." - John 10:27*

Narrator: "Before He died, Jesus told His followers that He would not leave them orphans but would send them the Holy Spirit to be their helper."

Action: Jesus continues to mouth words to His followers and the followers look like they are listening and engaged.

Scripture: *"If you love Me, keep My commandments. And I will pray the Father, and He will give you another Helper, that He may abide with you forever— the Spirit of truth, whom the world cannot receive, because it neither sees Him nor knows Him; but you know Him, for He dwells with you and will be in you. I will not leave you orphans; I will come to you." - John 14:15-18*

"But the Helper, the Holy Spirit, whom the Father will send in My name, He will teach you all things, and bring to your remembrance all things that I said to you." - John 14:26

Narrator: "Jesus died on the cross and, count with me (have the audience count with you), **on the one, two, three, third day, He rose from the grave!"**

Action: Jesus acts out dying on a cross, laying down as if being buried, and, as the audience counts to three, He jumps to display rising again.

Narrator: "After His resurrection Jesus appeared to His disciples and breathed into them the Holy Spirit, just like God breathed into Adam at creation."

Action: Jesus acts out breathing on the believers. Holy Spirit comes around them and motions as if coming <u>inside</u> of them. Holy Spirit now stays, standing behind the believers for the rest of the time, possibly motioning softly with his/her arms.

Scripture: *So Jesus said to them again, "Peace to you! As the Father has sent Me, I also send you." And when He had said this, He breathed on them, and said to them, "Receive the Holy Spirit. If you forgive the sins of any, they are forgiven them; if you retain the sins of any, they are retained." - John 20:21-23*

Narrator: "Before going back to heaven, Jesus told His followers to wait in Jerusalem for the Holy Spirit to come upon them."

Action: Jesus keeps talking to the believers as they listen and then steps back into line.

Scripture: *And being assembled together with them, He commanded them not to depart from Jerusalem, but to wait for the Promise of the Father, "which," He said, "you have heard from Me; for John truly baptized with water, but you shall be baptized with the Holy Spirit not many days from now." Therefore, when they had come together, they asked Him, saying, "Lord, will You at this time restore the kingdom to Israel?" And He said to them, "It is not for you to know times or seasons which the Father has put in His own authority. But you shall receive power when the Holy Spirit has come upon you; and you shall be witnesses to Me in Jerusalem, and in all Judea and Samaria, and to the end of the earth." - Acts 1:4-8*

Narrator: "On the day of Pentecost, many believers were gathered together when there was a sound like a rushing wind. Tongues of fire came upon their heads, and they began to speak in different languages. Peter spoke up and said this meant that God was now pouring out the Holy Spirit on all people and that this also meant that all believers can now prophesy."

Action: Holy Spirit acts out coming upon the believers. Believers use their hands like tongues on their heads. Peter steps out, faces the believers, and mouths words and motions as if to talk to them and explain what is happening.

Scripture: "When the Day of Pentecost had fully come, they were all with one accord in one place. And suddenly there came a sound from heaven, as of a rushing mighty wind, and it filled the whole house where they were sitting. Then there appeared to them divided tongues, as of fire, and one sat upon each of them. And they were all filled with the Holy Spirit and began to speak with other tongues, as the Spirit gave them utterance." - Acts 2:1-4

"But this is what was spoken by the prophet Joel: 'And it shall come to pass in the last days, says God, That I will pour out My Spirit on all flesh; Your sons and your daughters shall prophesy, Your young men shall see visions, Your old men shall dream dreams. And on My menservants and on My maidservants I will pour out My Spirit in those days; And they shall prophesy.'" - Acts 2:16-18

Action: Peter steps back in line.

Narrator: "Paul told us that there are many different gifts of the Holy Spirit. Each gift is given for the benefit of everyone, but love is the most important."

Action: Paul steps out, faces the believers, and mouths words as if talking to them.

Scripture: "Now concerning spiritual gifts, brethren, I do not want you to be ignorant . . . But the manifestation of the Spirit is given to each one for the profit of all: for to one is given the word of wisdom through the Spirit, to another the word of knowledge through the same Spirit, to another faith by the same Spirit, to another gifts of healings by the same Spirit, to another the working of miracles, to another prophecy, to another discerning of spirits, to another different kinds of tongues, to another the interpretation of tongues."
- 1 Corinthians 12:1,7-10

"And though I have the gift of prophecy, and understand all mysteries and all knowledge, and though I have all faith, so that I could remove mountains, but have not love, I am nothing." - 1 Corinthians 13:2

Narrator: "Paul told believers that they should pursue love, desire spiritual gifts, and especially desire to prophesy."

Action: Paul continues to mouth words and move his hands to the believers who look like they are listening. The believers act out being loving toward each other.

Scripture: "Pursue love, and desire spiritual gifts, but especially that you may prophesy."
- 1 Corinthians 14:1

Narrator: "He said that people who prophesy speak to others to strengthen them, encourage them, and comfort them and that everyone can prophesy, one at a time, so everyone is encouraged."

Action: As Paul talks, the believers mouth words at each other as if to talk. Some believers talk and some listen, and they all look very encouraged.

Scripture: *"But the one who prophesies speaks to people for their strengthening, encouraging and comfort." - 1 Corinthians 14:3*

"For you can all prophesy one by one, that all may learn and all may be encouraged." - 1 Corinthians 14:31

Narrator: "This is unlike the Old Testament, where only special people had the Holy Spirit come upon them in power, only Prophets could speak on behalf of God, and only Priests had special access to God for the people."

Action: The Prophet and Priest step out and Holy Spirit acts out coming upon them. The Prophet stands in front of Father God, as Father God mouths words, and the Prophet looks like he is speaking on God's behalf to the believers. The Priest looks like he is listening to one of the believers and then going back and forth between God and them on their behalf.

Narrator: "In the New Testament, all believers can have the Holy Spirit come upon them in power. This is called the baptism or the filling of the Spirit. Now all believers can connect with God directly, hear His voice, and prophesy!"

Action: The Prophet and Priest step back with the believers. Holy Spirit acts out coming upon all believers. Father God mouths words and all the believers get excited. They nod to show they understand and then they begin to mouth words and act out sharing what they have heard with each other.

END This is a great place to end the skit. If you feel like your group needs a little more clarity, you can add on the additional part below. Wherever you finish, make sure to thank your volunteers and have them take a bow.

Narrator: "While all believers can prophesy, not all believers are Prophets. A major role for Prophets in the New Testament is to help God's people to hear His voice for themselves directly and to have a healthy prophetic ministry to others."

Action: The Prophet goes around and acts out helping each of the believers to be better able to hear God for themselves and share healthy words with others.

Scripture: *And He Himself gave some to be apostles, some prophets, some evangelists, and some pastors and teachers, for the equipping of the saints for the work of ministry, for the edifying of the body of Christ . . . - Ephesians 4:11-12*

Narrator: "We should not be concerned about trying to figure out if we are a Prophet or any other type of leader or not. If you think you are called to church leadership, other responsible leaders will confirm that. Mature believers NEVER brag about a title or status or try to make others follow them. As believers we should each seek to be filled with the Holy Spirit and also seek the gifts of the Spirit, including growing in our ability to prophesy over others. A healthy Christian and prophetic culture will result in the fruit of the Spirit which is love, joy, peace, long-suffering, kindness, goodness, faithfulness, gentleness, and self-control."

Kingdom Creativity

In the beginning God created the heavens and the earth . . . Then God said, "Let Us make man in Our image, according to Our likeness. . . So God created man in His own image."
- Genesis 1:1, 26a, 27a

Out of the ground the Lord God formed every beast of the field and every bird of the air, and brought them to Adam to see what he would call them. And whatever Adam called each living creature, that was its name. - Genesis 2:19

Then the Lord spoke to Moses, saying: "See, I have called by name Bezalel the son of Uri, the son of Hur, of the tribe of Judah. And I have filled him with the Spirit of God, in wisdom, in understanding, in knowledge, and in all manner of workmanship, to design artistic works, to work in gold, in silver, in bronze, in cutting jewels for setting, in carving wood, and to work in all manner of workmanship. And I, indeed I, have appointed with him Aholiab the son of Ahisamach, of the tribe of Dan; and I have put wisdom in the hearts of all the gifted artisans, that they may make all that I have commanded you."
- Exodus 31:1-6

God is the Creator and because we are His kids, that means we are creative too! Just like in Acts chapter two when the people each heard the word of God in their own heart language, kingdom creativity speaks to our hearts and also to the heart languages of all those around us. When we create from a place of encounter with the Lord, our creation continues to release a God encounter for others. We can be creative in any area of our lives from the arts, to music, gardening, cooking, leadership, business, raising families, technology, and more!

Just like Adam did in naming the animals, we can actually co-create with God. Just as the artists were the first people in the Bible to be filled with the Spirit, so we can bring our creative talents before the Lord and use them to display on the earth what is happening in heaven. Kingdom creativity sees from heaven's perspective, creates new realities on the earth, releases creative miracles, and finds solutions to difficult problems.

In this section we will look at some basic principles for receiving and releasing kingdom creativity.

Resources
Cultivating Kingdom Creativity by Theresa Dedmon, TheresaDedmon.com
Sounds of the Nations Institute with Dano McCollam, SoundsOfTheNations.com
Evergreen Missions with Caleb and Gladys Byerly, EvergreenMissions.com

Creative Identity

Scripture
For You formed my inward parts; You covered me in my mother's womb. I will praise You, for I am fearfully and wonderfully made; marvelous are Your works, and that my soul knows very well. My frame was not hidden from You, when I was made in secret, and skillfully wrought in the lowest parts of the earth. Your eyes saw my substance, being yet unformed. And in Your book they all were written, the days fashioned for me, when as yet there were none of them. - Psalm 139:13-16

Description
God sees us and has known us from before we were born up to our current, everyday lives. It is important that we also see ourselves and those around us the way that God sees us. When we can communicate identity in a creative way it powerfully and uniquely impacts our hearts.

Activation 1
- Ask the Lord to show you how He sees you and create a picture of what He showed you.

Activation 2
- Partner up with someone else and ask the Lord to show each of you how He sees the other person. Draw a picture of what He shows you.
- Explain the pictures that you each drew for one another.
- Share with your partner what the Lord showed you about yourself in Activation 1. Compare what God showed you about yourself with what He showed your partner about you.

Activations 3+
Ask the Lord for a word of encouragement for yourself or someone else or to show you how He sees you or them. Share the word through one or more of the ways below. You can start with the prophetic word and share it creatively or share something creatively and then ask the Lord for an encouraging word to go with what you just did.
- Name acrostic (Write a prophetic/encouraging word for each letter of their name.)
- Photograph (Give a photograph with a prophetic word about the picture. Or point to an image on your phone or nearby and share what it means.)
- A simple drawing with one word (This could be a stick person or very basic drawing.)
- Painting (Paint a picture or ask the Lord what color, shape, or texture you/they are like.)
- Writing or poem (Write a short story, creative writing, poem, paragraph, etc.)
- Sound (Release a sound with your voice or other instrument and share what it means.)
- Song (Sing a known song with a prophetic meaning or ask the Lord to give you a new or prophetic song to sing.)
- Dance or movement (This can be simple movements or any type of dance.)
- Action (Do a prophetic act, like jumping up and down to release joy.)

Application
Ask the Lord regularly how He sees you and find creative ways to process and release what He shows you. Reach out to others and do the same thing! Consider emailing, texting, or mailing prophetic pictures to others or even leaving one for your server at a restaurant.

Creative Problem Solving

Scripture
So he went with them. And when they came to the Jordan, they cut down trees. But as one was cutting down a tree, the iron ax head fell into the water; and he cried out and said, "Alas, master! For it was borrowed." So the man of God said, "Where did it fall?" And he showed him the place. So he cut off a stick, and threw it in there; and he made the iron float. Therefore he said, "Pick it up for yourself." So he reached out his hand and took it.
- 2 Kings 6:4-7

Description
Oftentimes we are faced with problems that we have no earthly idea how to solve. Partnering with Holy Spirit to get wisdom (knowing what to do) and revelation will lead us to creative solutions to difficult problems.

Activation
- Write down a specific problem in your life that you don't know what to do about.
- Ask God for wisdom for what to do.
- Now stop thinking about that problem and instead on a piece of paper, draw a mountain.
- Draw yourself on one side of the mountain.
- Next, draw a creative way that you are going to get over that mountain.
  - E.g. fly, tunnel, ride a train, go on a water slide, etc.
- Then draw yourself on the other side of the mountain.
- Share your drawing and how you got over the mountain with a partner.
- Now look back at your problem again and see if you have a creative solution.
- If so, share your problem and solution with your partner.
- Pray for each other and for the solutions for your problems.

Application
When you're faced with a difficult problem ask the Lord for wisdom and then put your problem aside and do something creative. As you stop focusing on the issue and open yourself up for creative solutions, you'll often find yourself getting an answer that you hadn't thought of before.

*Lesson inspired by Pastor Jamey VanGelder, The House Church

Societal Transformation

Who has heard such a thing? Who has seen such things? Shall the earth be made to give birth in one day? Or shall a nation be born at once? For as soon as Zion was in labor, she gave birth to her children. – Isaiah 66:8

Simon Peter answered and said, "You are the Christ, the Son of the living God." . . . "And I also say to you that you are Peter, and on this rock I will build My church, and the gates of Hades shall not prevail against it. And I will give you the keys of the kingdom of heaven, and whatever you bind on earth will be bound in heaven, and whatever you loose on earth will be loosed in heaven." - Matthew 16:16,18-19

"You are the salt of the earth; . . . You are the light of the world. A city that is set on a hill cannot be hidden. Nor do they light a lamp and put it under a basket, but on a lampstand, and it gives light to all who are in the house. Let your light so shine before men, that they may see your good works and glorify your Father in heaven." - Matthew 5:13a,14-16

Then the men of the city said to Elisha, "Please notice, the situation of this city is pleasant, as my lord sees; but the water is bad, and the ground barren." And he said, "Bring me a new bowl, and put salt in it." So they brought it to him. Then he went out to the source of the water, and cast in the salt there, and said, "Thus says the Lord: 'I have healed this water; from it there shall be no more death or barrenness.'" - 2 Kings 2:19-21

As believers in Jesus we are His Church and His body on the earth. In addition to going to church and inviting others to attend with us, we have the opportunity to be salt and light to people outside the walls of our church buildings. We can be people like Daniel, Joseph, and Nehemiah who add value to even unrighteous leaders and help build up society at large.

What would it look like if instead of only asking the world to come to church, we brought the unconditional love, hope, and acceptance of Jesus to each area of society that we have influence in and simply served them like Jesus came to serve us? As the salt of the earth, what if we looked to bring out the wonderful God flavor that is already in the people and places of the world all around us? What if we looked for the "gates of hell" in our communities and went there to bring healing and hope?

Throughout Scripture, key individuals stand out for the way their lives affected their society. In this section, we will examine aspects of their lives and other key principles to see how we too can bring change to not only other believers, but to society as a whole.

Adam and Eve: Having Dominion

Scripture
Then God blessed them, and God said to them, "Be fruitful and multiply; fill the earth and subdue it; have dominion over the fish of the sea, over the birds of the air, and over every living thing that moves on the earth". . Then the Lord God took the man and put him in the garden of Eden to tend and keep it. - Genesis 1:28; 2:15

Description
God told Adam and Eve to be in charge of the whole earth and then He put them in a contained environment: a garden. The idea was that little by little, men and women would extend the garden until the whole earth looked like heaven. The same is true in our lives today. The Lord tells us to change the world, but we all have a place of Eden where we need to start. We need to be faithful with where we are currently and trust that as we steward what we have well, it will grow and expand.

Just like a dot on a map cannot tell us where we are without other points of reference (e.g. latitude and longitude lines) so we as individuals need the context of other people to live out who God calls us to be. We can think of the latitude lines (the ones going left and right) as the story of God's people throughout time, and the longitude lines (going up and down) as the story of our people in our time. We each have key people from the Bible and history whom the Lord highlights to us. We also have key relationships in our lives right now that are important for us to be connected to generationally.

Activation
- Say, "Lord, speak to me and lead me as we do this together."
- Get out a blank piece of paper and draw a dot in the middle of the page. This is you.
- To the left and right of your dot write the names of people in the Bible, in history, or who are alive today who you feel that the Lord is highlighting for you to learn from.
- Think about the people in your life who you are relationally connected to right now and who are important to your journey. Write the names of father or mother figures under your dot (because their ceiling is your floor), peer relationships next to your dot, and son or daughter type relationships above your dot (because your ceiling is their floor).
- Now draw the biggest circle that you can fit on the page. This represents the world. On that circle write some of the big things that you feel called to or want to do with your life.
- Between your dot and the big circle, draw a small to medium circle. This represents your Eden. In this circle write some words that represent your life right now.
- What do you need to do now to take better care of yourself, your relationships, or your Eden before you try to expand it? Write that down on your paper.
- Draw some arrows going out from your smaller circle to the big circle. Ask the Lord to show you what it will look like for you to expand where you are now to where you feel you are supposed to go. Write what He shows you on the arrows.
  - E.g. Maybe on your big circle you write that you want to be president but in your Eden circle you write that you are currently in tenth grade. In your Eden circle you may write "Get better grades." On your arrows you may write things like, "Volunteer in my community." Or, "Run for school government."

Application
It is important for us to have big dreams, callings, and goals. It is also important to be honest about where we are currently. As we faithfully steward what we have now, it will grow into something bigger. If we can see how where we are now will be a part of where we are going, it will be easier for us to work hard and not try to take shortcuts. The big dreams we have will always need other people and may take generations to come to pass.

* Lesson inspired by Pastor Jamey VanGelder, The House Church

Abraham: Seeking Mercy Not Judgment

Scripture
And Abraham came near and said, "Would You also destroy the righteous with the wicked? Suppose there were fifty righteous within the city; would You also destroy the place and not spare it for the fifty righteous that were in it? Far be it from You to do such a thing as this, to slay the righteous with the wicked, so that the righteous should be as the wicked; far be it from You! Shall not the Judge of all the earth do right?" - Genesis 18:23-25

Description
When Abraham found out that judgment was coming to Sodom and Gomorrah he did not pronounce destruction. Instead, he interceded before God for the city to be spared. Had Abraham continued with the prayer that he started, the city may have been saved. Many people today are speaking words of judgment against different places and people groups in the world. However, this passage shows us that we should instead pray and do everything in our power for people's lives to be spared.

We can talk with the Lord as a friend and affect the outcome of world events. If it seems that harm will come to a people or place, we should stand in a place of prayer and release mercy and not judgment.

Activation
- Write out the names of several groups of people or places that have a lot of judgment against them. This could include specific nations or neighborhoods as well as ethnic, religious, economic, or social groups.
- Spend time talking with the Lord about each group or place and releasing mercy and love to them.
- Ask the Lord if there are any specific ways you can pray for and release life to each group or place.

Application
The Lord wants to release mercy. Jesus didn't come to condemn the world but to save it (John 3:15-17). As believers, we too need to seek ways for all people to be saved.

Joseph: Solutions to Problems

Scripture

So the advice was good in the eyes of Pharaoh and in the eyes of all his servants. And Pharaoh said to his servants, "Can we find such a one as this, a man in whom is the Spirit of God?" Then Pharaoh said to Joseph, "Inasmuch as God has shown you all this, there is no one as discerning and wise as you. You shall be over my house, and all my people shall be ruled according to your word; only in regard to the throne will I be greater than you." And Pharaoh said to Joseph, "See, I have set you over all the land of Egypt." - Genesis 41:37-41

But as for you, you meant evil against me; but God meant it for good, in order to bring it about as it is this day, to save many people alive. - Genesis 50:20

Description

Joseph interpreted the dreams of Pharaoh, predicting future world events and giving direction for how to prepare for what was ahead. Because of this, Pharaoh put him in charge of executing this plan, which Joseph did for the next fourteen years. Joseph not only saved Egypt, but all of the known world at the time. He also saved his family, with whom he was ultimately restored. Joseph was connected to heaven, saw what was ahead, worked with world leaders, and provided solutions for problems that otherwise would have devastated society.

What if you were fearless to look at both your current situation and the future and with God's help, could foresee major issues? Then, what if you used a skill set that you already have to share the solution so that the problem didn't seem so bad? What if you were then able to work alongside other leaders, overseeing the implementation of the solution? What if you did this in such a way that even in times of trouble, you brought increased favor and honor to those you worked for and you and your family benefited personally?

Activation

Compare your life and Joseph's life in the following areas. Write down the answers to the questions below on a separate piece of paper.

Joseph	You
Saw clearly what the problem was: the world would go into famine.	**See**: What is a problem that you see? (Anything from a global issue to a problem at work, in the present or the future.)
Skill: used a skill he was good at that got his foot in the door: Dream Interpretation.	**Skill**: What skill are you good at that will gain you favor with leaders in this area?
Solved it: Provided the solution: Save up food then sell it back.	**Solution**: What is a solution to the problem?
Spearheaded it: Personally oversaw the implementation of the solution.	**Spearhead**: How would you, personally, implement the solution?
Succeeded personally as well as publicly: Was reconciled to his family.	**Success** personally: How will this also be a blessing to you and your family?

Solomon: Wisdom in the Details

Scripture

And when the queen of Sheba had seen all the wisdom of Solomon, the house that he had built, the food on his table, the seating of his servants, the service of his waiters and their apparel, his cupbearers, and his entryway by which he went up to the house of the Lord, there was no more spirit in her. Then she said to the king: "It was a true report which I heard in my own land about your words and your wisdom. However I did not believe the words until I came and saw with my own eyes; and indeed the half was not told me. Your wisdom and prosperity exceed the fame of which I heard." - 1 Kings 10:4-7

Description

The Queen of Sheba came from far away to see the wisdom of Solomon. In the end it was his excellence in the little things (the food on his table, the seating of his servants, the service of his waiters and their apparel, his cupbearers, and his entryway) that made her believe there was a God in Israel.

What if we could impact nations by having extreme wisdom and excellence in how we do the small things of life? What if the Lord gave you an invention that made a daily routine (like eating or sleeping) even better? What if He gave you a new way to make food or design clothing? What if peace between nations came because of the way you did interior decorating or the way you built houses?

Activation

- Get out a piece of paper and write the following areas from this passage on it, putting circles around each word. You'll be making a "web" on the page, so leave room around each word or feel free to use several pages if you'd like.
    - Architecture
    - Culinary Arts
    - Food Service
    - Administration
    - Customer Service
    - Fashion
    - Interior Design
- From each phrase draw lines and write more areas of influence that could be included within each topic. E.g. For culinary arts you could put "agriculture, chef, farmer, food safety," etc.
- Mark the areas that you feel called to on your page. If the area(s) you are called to aren't on the page yet, go ahead and add them.
- Ask the Lord for wisdom in your area(s), that you would be so excellent in your realm of influence the world would know the Lord is God.
- Write down what the Lord shows you and share it with a partner.

Application

Daily ask God for wisdom in your areas of expertise. Know that every little thing, done excellently, will bring God glory.

Societal Transformation - 117

The Seven Mountains of Society

Scripture
Now it shall come to pass in the latter days that the mountain of the Lord's house shall be established on the top of the mountains, and shall be exalted above the hills; and all nations shall flow to it. - Isaiah 2:2

"You are the light of the world. A city that is set on a hill cannot be hidden." - Matthew 5:14

Description
As we are called to make disciples of all nations, we have the ability to not only disciple individuals but also entire people groups, countries, and even areas of society. One way to picture the different areas of society is to think of them as seven mountains or seven areas of influence. As Christians, we are called to not only be salt and light and influence people in the church, but also in all areas of society. Being a stay at home parent is just as important as being a business leader or a pastor. The church is very important, but it is only one of the seven areas. If we know the main mountain(s) we are called to influence, we can more intentionally grow in practical skills to serve that realm of society. The idea of the seven mountains of society was originally developed by the founders of Youth With a Mission (YWAM), Loren Cunningham, and Bill Bright of Campus Crusade for Christ.

The seven mountains of society are:
1. **Religion:** including the church as well as all religions.
2. **Family:** including marriage, adoption, tribes, and all values or roles connected to family.
3. **Education:** including all forms of school, universities, internships, etc.
4. **Government:** including all politics, law, courts, military, police, elected officials, etc.
5. **Media:** including all news, magazines, newspapers, internet communication, etc.
6. **Arts & Entertainment:** also called "celebration." This includes all movies, TV, music, theater, sports, social media, and all forms of creative expression.
7. **Business:** including all forms of economics, markets, commerce, science, technology, farming, human trafficking, illegal business, etc.

Healthcare can be in family, business, or even other mountains.

Activation
- Draw and label the seven mountains. Draw yourself on the mountain(s) that you are currently influencing. Write down how you are influencing that area.
- Ask the Lord out loud, "Lord, which of the mountains are You calling me to influence?"
- If it is one you are not currently influencing, draw yourself on that mountain.
- Ask out loud, "Lord, how do You want me to be a kingdom influencer in this area?"
- Write down what He shows you and share it with a partner.

Application
When we know our realm of authority we can live more intentionally and make a greater impact on the world around us.

Resources
LanceWallnau.com, Generals.org

Prayer Evangelism

Scripture
. . . pray without ceasing. - 1 Thessalonians 5:17

Every place that the sole of your foot will tread upon I have given you. - Joshua 1:3a

But whatever house you enter, first say, "Peace to this house." And if a son of peace is there, your peace will rest on it; if not, it will return to you. - Luke 10:5-6

"You shall love your neighbor as yourself." - Galatians 5:14b

The prayer of a righteous person is powerful and effective - Jame 5:16b (NIV)

Description
Most moves of God first began with prayer. As the Moravians prayed in Germany for 100 years, they launched the biggest missions movement the world had yet seen, eventually being a catalyst for the Great Awakening in America. As the Celts in Ireland prayed for 300 years starting at Bangor Abbey, they became a missions movement throughout all of Europe. We do not need to pray for this long or even go a long ways away to see transformation take place. Helping others experience the kingdom of God can be as simple as choosing a small group of people that we live, work, or go to school with and consistently praying for them. We can speak words of peace, blessing, and life over them and look for ways to build a relationship. As we get to know them, we can find out what is going on in their lives, encourage them, and minister to their felt needs. As they experience the kingdom, there will eventually be opportunities to share the Gospel with them and invite them to surrender their lives to Jesus. Then we can continue to journey with them and disciple them.

Activation 1 - Speak Peace and Blessing
- Intentionally speak words of life, peace, and blessing when you talk to or about the people and places in your life.

Activation 2 - Adopt Your Neighbors
- Adopt the two to five houses (apartments, cubicles, lockers, etc.) to your left, the two to five to your right, and the five to ten across from you. Intentionally pray for those people on a regular basis. (E.g. Consider getting in your car five minutes early each morning and praying for your neighbors before you leave.)
- Intentionally build relationships with those neighbors and look for ways to encourage and minister to their needs.

Activation 3 - Prayer Walk
- Once a week, go for a walk around your neighborhood (and/or school, workplace, etc.). As you go pray for the people, houses, offices, situations, etc. in the area. Speak blessings and peace over the people, land, buildings, and circumstances.
- You can do this alone or with your believing friends, neighbors, or family members.

Application
As you do this, you will begin to see individuals and families impacted for the kingdom. As you build relationships and your neighbors come to know the Lord, consider opening up your home, office, or a classroom for regular gatherings to fellowship and disciple them.

Resources
Lesson inspired by Ed Silvoso, see the book *Prayer Evangelism* and other books and resources on TransformOurWorld.org

Societal Transformation - 119

Pray for and Honor Leaders

Scripture
Therefore I exhort first of all that supplications, prayers, intercessions, and giving of thanks be made for all men, for kings and all who are in authority, that we may lead a quiet and peaceable life in all godliness and reverence. - 1 Timothy 2:1-2

Let every soul be subject to the governing authorities. For there is no authority except from God, and the authorities that exist are appointed by God. - Romans 13:1

The king's heart is in the hand of the Lord, like the rivers of water; He turns it wherever He wishes. - Proverbs 21:1

Description
Paul tells us to be thankful for, subject to, and spend time in prayer for all those in authority. We must be careful to not curse our leaders, but instead to look for areas where we can be thankful for them and bless them. We should honor our leaders the same way we honor the Lord. We don't give honor because people deserve it. We give honor because we are honorable people and honor is what kingdom people do.

Activation
- Make a list of the leaders in your life: your manager, pastor, city leaders, national leaders, etc.
- Thank the Lord for each one of them and pray for them by name.
- If there is an area where you are frustrated with them, choose to bless them instead of curse them. Declare Proverbs 21:1 (listed above) over them.
- Ask the Lord to show you what is on His heart for each of them and declare over them what is true in heaven about them.
- If you are in relationship with any of them, ask the Lord if there are any words of encouragement that He would have you to share with them.

Application
Whenever you see something negative about a leader, take a moment to pray for and bless them. Declare the kingdom of heaven over their lives and that they would have great wisdom as they lead. Be intentional to honor those in authority over you just as you honor the Lord.

Two Ways to See the World

We have been on a powerful journey together throughout these many pages. The two final lessons in this book relate to two different ways of seeing the world, also called worldviews.

The model called the "Traditional Christian Worldview" illustrates how many believers see the world, their families, leaders, church, and the Lord. Many are waiting for Jesus to come back and rescue them. Others are simply trying to manage their sin, be good Christians, and go to church. Many believers are trying to get the world into the church building, and believe it is okay to put ministry before their personal health or families. In this model, believers see more programs, church activities, and meetings as the primary way to release the kingdom of God on the earth. In this model, church leaders are often set apart as the only ones who can do ministry, while the people around them are primarily there to serve their vision. Because God always honors His word (Isaiah 55), there will still be fruit from this model. However, it does not demonstrate the way we see the kingdom of God in the New Testament.

The second model called the "Kingdom Worldview" shows a very different perspective. In fact it is the exact opposite! In this model, believers recognize the kingdom of God is already here and that it begins inside of them. This brings us back to the Garden of Eden we discussed at the very beginning of the book. In this model we start with an understanding of the goodness of God and we begin to grow His kingdom, or His garden, on the inside of us. Just like in Genesis, this kingdom then expands little by little until it covers the whole world. After getting the kingdom in us, we cultivate it and begin to expand it to those closest to us, like our spouse, children, and close friends. Little by little the kingdom of God expands until we are able to reach our neighbors, co-workers, and even the ends of the earth. In the second model we understand that our families are more important than ministry or work, that our neighborhoods and workplaces are our missions fields, that our work is holy, and that we can change the world by starting at home.

Please read and pray through the two different worldview pictures on the following pages before continuing on to the final two lessons. It is best to read the non-kingdom worldview from the top down and the kingdom worldview from the bottom up. Please note that there are additional verses at the end of this section that provide even more scriptural background on the kingdom worldview model.

Traditional Christian Worldview

**God is distant and displeased.
We experience heaven only when we die.**

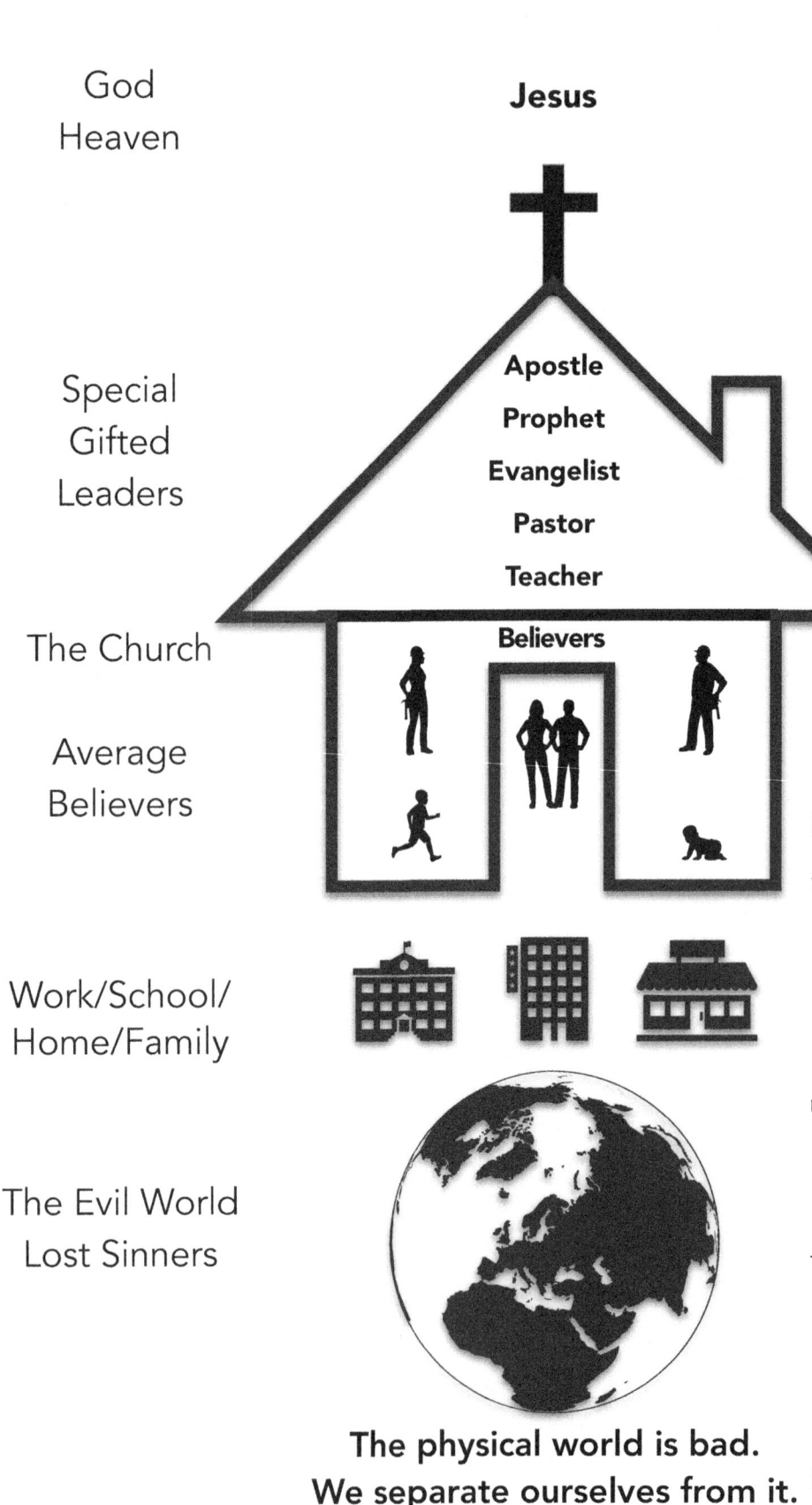

God
Heaven

Jesus

Apostle
Prophet
Evangelist
Pastor
Teacher

Believers

Special
Gifted
Leaders

The Church

Average
Believers

Work/School/
Home/Family

The Evil World
Lost Sinners

**The physical world is bad.
We separate ourselves from it.**

God is high above us, far off, and often displeased with us. As believers, we want God to come down and help us. We are waiting for Jesus to return in order for things to get better instead of feeling responsible to bring change now. We are waiting to experience heaven when we die.

God chooses special people to help us get closer to Him. They have more favor and connection to Him. The higher the title, the closer they are to God. They are the experts from whom we need permission when making personal life decisions.

Churches are buildings with large weekly gatherings, usually run by adult male leaders, with many programs and services.

Church ministry is our highest priority. As believers we are to serve our church leaders, spend as much time as possible in church, and help other people come to church events to learn how to live rightly.

Our work, school, home, and neighborhood is not as important as ministry. It is okay to prioritize ministry over our marriage, children, family, and personal health. Children and young people do not have as much value as adults.

The world is lost, evil, and going to hell. We must stay pure from its affects and help to save it. Many things in our culture, like music, movies, or technology are evil and must be avoided and rejected. As believers it is our job to tell people in the world how to live.

Kingdom Worldview

God made the world, so it is good.

We engage the world and release heaven on earth now.

Heaven on earth now and society transformed

Empowered and equipped believers reach their neighbors, co-workers, and areas of influence, mostly outside of the church building

Churches gather people to fellowship, equip, and send them out

Leaders lay down their lives so believers can reach the world

Personal relationship with God and family

We start with the understanding of God's presence, love, and goodness to us personally and the whole world

Acts 1:8

Ends of the Earth

Judea / Samaria

Jerusalem

Receiving Holy Spirit

Believers

Teacher
Pastor
Evangelist
Prophet
Apostle

I am a mom, dad, husband, wife, son, daughter, etc.

Identity in earthly family

I am a son of God

Identity in God's family

Jesus

God is good and loving.

We can experience heaven now.

The world is destined to look like heaven. Believers serve the world and lay down our lives to lift others up.

Believers take responsibility for our neighborhoods, work places, and schools as our ministry and mission fields. We are commissioned to go into every area of society (religion, family, education, government, media, arts and entertainment, and business). We release heaven on earth through our everyday lives, wherever we have influence.

Believers gather in church buildings for fellowship, teaching, and equipping, and then are sent out into the world. Churches can be large, small, house churches, or even businesses, schools, or any other gathering and sending community of people. They can be led by men or women and even younger people.

Leaders lay down their lives to serve. Their role is to equip others so that those they are connected with can walk in the grace that they, as a leader, carry. Leaders trust their people to make wise choices. They share wise counsel and value relational connection. They focus more on commissioning their people rather than needing them to get their permission to do what they sense God is calling them to do.

After our relationship with Jesus, our family is our highest priority. The younger generation is connected to the older and the older lifts up the younger to go further than themselves. We care for our physical, mental, and emotional health.

Jesus died to reconcile all people back to the Father. As believers we live in constant relationship with Him.

We start by living from heavenly places. God is good, He is always with us, and dearly loves us!

Societal Transformation - 123

Equipped and Equipping

Scripture
And He Himself gave some to be apostles, some prophets, some evangelists, and some pastors and teachers, for the equipping of the saints for the work of ministry, for the edifying of the body of Christ. - Ephesians 4:11-12

Description
The work of Christian leaders is not primarily to DO ministry but to EQUIP average believers to do the work of ministry. When leaders are functioning in their proper order, their people will be healthy and able to walk in the same type of grace as the leader. Like a good father is happy to see his son take on the family business, secure leaders are happy to see their people run farther than them. Building upon the foundation of Jesus, leaders are able to lay down their lives to be the foundation that other believers build their lives upon. While not everyone is called to the formal office of the five areas listed in Ephesians 4, we are ALL called to be equipped to be apostolic, prophetic, evangelistic, pastoral, and able to share kingdom truths with others. If you are called to any type of formal leadership it is not something that you seek or appoint yourself to, but rather something that others in authority in that office would call and set you into.

Apostles help people live by, and create around them, the culture of heaven. Apostles were Roman generals sent to show conquered people how to live like Romans. When Jesus used this term His followers knew that it meant they were to help those around them live according to the kingdom of heaven. Prophets not only speak the revealed word of the Lord, but are also there to make sure that everyone in their environment can hear from God and minister in a healthy prophetic culture for themselves. Evangelists are not only given to win the lost themselves, but to help the average believer have a value for and a toolset to bring lost sons and daughters home. Pastors not only care for the sheep, but also create a healthy environment where people in the body can care for one another. Lastly, teachers not only teach the Word of God, but also help each believer know how to understand the Word of God for themselves and share it with others. All of these areas and expressions are not limited only to church meetings.

Activation 1
- Write or share the following with a partner.
- Based on the descriptions above, how can you more intentionally live a life that is apostolic, prophetic, evangelistic, pastoral, and able to teach others?

Activation 2
- Read the "Two Ways to See the World" in this section and the two models that follow.
- Based on the kingdom worldview model, what are some ways that you can both serve and equip those you are leading (whether in the church or in family or in business)?

Application
We will always need leaders in our lives and should submit to their authority, but it is the responsibility of each one of us to do the work of ministry. This requires each believer to mature and grow up into all that God has for them. As a mature believer I am equipped and empowered to heal the sick, save the lost, hear from God for myself, and change the world around me! In areas where I lead I get to raise up those I lead and help them go further than I have ever gone so that my ceiling is their floor.

Change the World, Start at Home

Scripture
Your kingdom come. Your will be done on earth as it is in heaven. - Matthew 6:10

But you shall receive power when the Holy Spirit has come upon you; and you shall be witnesses to Me in Jerusalem, and in all Judea and Samaria, and to the end of the earth. - Acts 1:8

And he has appointed some with grace to be apostles, and some with grace to be prophets, and some with grace to be evangelists, and some with grace to be pastors, and some with grace to be teachers. And their calling is to nurture and prepare all the holy believers to do their own works of ministry, and as they do this they will enlarge and build up the body of Christ - Ephesians 4:11-12 (TPT)

Description
In the beginning God made a good world with a perfect garden. This garden symbolized His kingdom on the earth. He put us, as His kids, in charge of caring for the garden and expanding it until it overtook the whole world. This assignment has never changed.

As God's kids it is our job to first get the kingdom of God inside of us and to walk in relationship with Him every single day (this is us personally receiving the Holy Spirit in power). Next we are responsible to live in right relationship and care for the people around us like our spouse, children, families, and close friends (this is our Jerusalem). After that our main mission field is our neighbors as well as our workplaces (this is our Judea and Samaria). Out of the overflow of bringing the kingdom in each of these areas we can then also reach the ends of the earth and see transformation come to all areas of society.

As believers we ARE the Church (with a big "C"), which means we are Jesus' body on the earth today. We also need to be a part of a local church (little "c") which is a community of people who gather regularly to fellowship, be equipped, and sent out to expand the kingdom of God to the world around them. Some people (not everyone) are given graces that Ephesians 4:11-16 says are designed to equip the rest of us to minister. These people, often appointed as leaders, are NOT to only do ministry but are to EQUIP believers to do ministry. We regularly gather with other believers in church to be equipped and sent out to bring heaven to earth in our daily lives. Just like most of Jesus' ministry happened outside of the temple, most of our ministry will happen outside of church.

Activation
- Read the "Two Ways to See the World" in this section and the two models that follow.
- Place a checkmark by the mindsets and experiences you currently have from each page.
- Talk with the Lord about where you are currently and where you would like to be.
- Read the kingdom Worldview model starting at the bottom and ask, "Lord, how do You want me to adjust to live more like Your kingdom?" Write down what He shows you.
- What are 1-3 practical things you can do this month to begin making those changes?
- Write down and share these things with a partner.

Application
As we embrace a kingdom worldview and intentionally live it out every day in our Jerusalem, Judea, and Samaria, we will change the world by starting at home.

Societal Transformation - 125

Scriptural Background for the Kingdom Worldview Model

Jesus announces the kingdom is here: *Now after John was put in prison, Jesus came to Galilee, preaching the gospel of the kingdom of God, and saying, "The time is fulfilled, and the kingdom of God is at hand. Repent, and believe in the gospel."* - Mark 1:14-15

And heal the sick there, and say to them, "The kingdom of God has come near to you." - Luke 10:9

Jesus didn't come to condemn, but to save the world: *For God so loved the world that He gave His only begotten Son, that whoever believes in Him should not perish but have everlasting life. For God did not send His Son into the world to condemn the world, but that the world through Him might be saved.* - John 3:16-17

Leaders are to equip believers: *And He Himself gave some to be apostles, some prophets, some evangelists, and some pastors and teachers, for the equipping of the saints for the work of ministry, for the edifying of the body of Christ, till we all come to the unity of the faith and of the knowledge of the Son of God, to a perfect man, to the measure of the stature of the fullness of Christ; that we should no longer be children, tossed to and fro and carried about with every wind of doctrine, by the trickery of men, in the cunning craftiness of deceitful plotting, but, speaking the truth in love, may grow up in all things into Him who is the head—Christ— from whom the whole body, joined and knit together by what every joint supplies, according to the effective working by which every part does its share, causes growth of the body for the edifying of itself in love.* - Ephesians 4:11-16

The gates of hell do not prevail against us (This means the Church as a people should be going to the gates of hell)**:** *And I also say to you that you are Peter, and on this rock I will build My church, and the gates of Hades shall not prevail against it. And I will give you the keys of the kingdom of heaven, and whatever you bind on earth will be bound in heaven, and whatever you loose on earth will be loosed in heaven."* - Matthew 16:18-19

The call to disciple nations: *And Jesus came and spoke to them, saying, "All authority has been given to Me in heaven and on earth. Go therefore and make disciples of all the nations, baptizing them in the name of the Father and of the Son and of the Holy Spirit, teaching them to observe all things that I have commanded you; and lo, I am with you always, even to the end of the age." Amen.* - Matthew 28:18-20

The call to be the salt of the earth (This means we need to influence people outside of our churches)**:** *"You are the salt of the earth; but if the salt loses its flavor, how shall it be seasoned? It is then good for nothing but to be thrown out and trampled underfoot by men."* - Matthew 5:13

Salt is used to heal the land of bitterness: *Then the men of the city said to Elisha, "Please notice, the situation of this city is pleasant, as my lord sees; but the water is bad, and the ground barren." And he said, "Bring me a new bowl, and put salt in it." So they brought it to him. Then he went out to the source of the water, and cast in the salt there, and said, "Thus says the Lord: 'I have healed this water; from it there shall be no more death or barrenness.'"* - 2 Kings 2:19-21

The Lord's prayer to see heaven on earth now: *In this manner, therefore, pray: Our Father in heaven, Hallowed be Your name. Your kingdom come. Your will be done On earth as it is in heaven.* - Matthew 6:9-10.

Facilitator's Guide

Anyone can facilitate a Kingdom Culture group. If you would like to use this material for a small group, event, with your family, in a classroom, homeschooling, or any other setting, this section has many pointers that will help you be successful. Kingdom Culture groups are being planted around the world and yours could be the next one. If you are interested in planting a Kingdom Culture School, please see our website for more information.

Being a Kingdom Culture Facilitator

What is a Facilitator?

- A facilitator helps guide people through an experience and is very different than a teacher or a preacher.
- They only talk as much as they need to.
- They allow others in the group to read parts of the lesson or share examples as is appropriate.
- A facilitator makes sure that people have enough understanding to participate in a lesson.
- If people need a personal testimony, example, or demonstration of a lesson they are able to do that.
- They can take the lead and not let any one person in the group dominate or take over.
- They are able to direct people if they get off topic or if they need help finding a partner.
- They help the group stay focused and on time.

As a Facilitator, You:

Create a Safe Place:
- While your role is to facilitate, you are still in charge and can adjust or direct what is happening in the group so that everyone feels safe. Safety looks like people feeling comfortable to share and feeling like they are listened to when they do. Safety also looks like not allowing any one person dominate a conversation or be so needy that the whole group is focused on them.

Stay Present:
- Like Mary sitting at Jesus' feet, if the Lord is doing something in a moment, feel free to stay there even if you don't get to all the things you had planned for your time.

Help People Move Along:
- Like a shepherd moving their sheep forward, you are still in charge and can direct and move people along. Without a shepherd, people tend to wander. Don't be afraid to keep people on topic, focus the conversation, or dismiss the group if it is getting late.

How to Facilitate a Kingdom Culture Group

Practical Pointers:

- **ANYONE can facilitate this!** All you have to do is lead the lesson, whether you or someone else reads it.
- Depending on your group, you can have volunteers read, or take turns reading the lessons out loud.
- Each lesson is designed to be a VERY SHORT "mini lesson" focused more on the learner than on the facilitator.
    - The goal is for participants to spend at least as much, if not more, time doing/activating the lesson and sharing with one another than they do listening to a teaching on it.
- **This material will work for anyone** who is hungry for God whether they do not yet know Him, are a new believer, or have been a believer for a long time. It is designed for those ages ten and up, and it is wonderful to do with multiple age groups interacting together. It can also work for younger children, but some lessons will need to be adjusted to their age level.
- **You can do each lesson with a group in about 15-20 minutes**, including activation time.
    - You can choose to have longer activation or partner/group sharing time. However, the goal is to keep the lessons moving forward. Focus on depth and momentum, and resist dragging. Do NOT preach.
- To give an overview of what you will be doing, you can read the cover title and the book tag line, or put it in your own words. For example, say, "Today we will be doing lessons from the *Kingdom Culture School of Ministry* manual. This course is designed to help us shift how we think, so we can change the world around us. We will do this by learning biblical truths that we can experience or activate in our daily lives."
- **When you first get started**, read the section about the Garden of Eden to your group, starting on page 2 and continue reading through, "Are You Living in the Kingdom of God?" on pages 3 - 4. Also read the "Getting Started" section on pages 11-12 to your group and remind the group of these guidelines whenever new people come. As long as people stay within these there isn't a right or a wrong answer.
- It is good to **read the chapter overview aloud** before starting to do lessons in that chapter.
- You can go through the book in order or choose your own order and start at any place.
- You have permission to adjust and use this book however works best for the people and the time that you have.
- Keep the atmosphere of your group light hearted, safe, and energetic.
- It is nice to provide paper and pencils/pens for people to do some of the activations or encourage them to bring their own.
- You can allow for more time at the end of your group for people to pray for one another.

Copyrights:

- Please do not photocopy this book. Please do encourage others to purchase their own copy. Proceeds from sales will fund ministry and translations in other nations.
- To purchase the rights to make additional small run copies please go to KristenDarpa.com.
- You can make small run copies of the following pages but please do not edit them in any way: "The Heart of an Orphan and The Heart of Sonship" (p. 21), "Soap and Three Crosses Examples" (p. 45), "15 second and 1-3 minute Testimony Example" (p. 71), "A Simple Way to Share the Gospel" (p. 73), "A Simple Salvation Prayer" (p. 75), "Four Ways to Grow" (p. 77), "Discipleship Model" (p. 79), "Treasure Hunts" (p. 81), and "Ways God Speaks" (p. 94).

Activation Pointers:

- When you share ground rules and guidelines at the beginning of this course, have your group **practice finding a new partner**. This is helpful to practice before you do the activations, so they can get used to doing this quickly. First, ask them to stand up, and then tell them to sit down once they have found a partner. They can ask each other their name and something fun like their favorite color, food, or the best part about their day. This helps people get used to the idea of interacting without it feeling scary.
- After this they can practice quickly finding a new partner and sharing something short again.
- For the sake of time, only have groups of two so that people have more time to share.
- Even if you are in a small group, if people always have a partner it guarantees that everyone will share and you can always take additional time to share with the small group as well. If they share once with a partner and once with the group it strengthens what they are learning.
- Even if you are in a larger group, depending on how much time you have, you can also have some people share with your whole group.
- It is good to **let people know how much time they will have** to do an activation (e.g. 3, 5, 8, 10 minutes). It is also helpful if you tell them when to switch, halfway through their time. That way, both partners have time to share.
- You may want to be prepared when you finish an activation to **help people transition** before starting the next lesson. Have everyone clap, cheer, stand up and sit down with a new partner, repeat something after you, etc.
- Whatever you do, make sure everyone has stopped talking before you continue on with the lesson.
- Consider playing upbeat music without lyrics softly in the background when doing the activations or in transitioning when the activations are done.

Helpful Things to Share or Model

- Bring the lessons to life for your audience by sharing a **short testimony** or example of how you have seen the topic lived out in your own experience.
- Often it is helpful to BRIEFLY **demonstrate**, model, or give an **example of an activation** so people can understand what you are asking them to do. For example, you could demonstrate giving a prophetic word, or show people a picture you drew of how you see God as being good to you personally.
- Be **authentic and appropriately vulnerable** with your group. For example, you could admit that sometimes you feel afraid to talk to strangers about Jesus, but you choose to do it anyway. People will feel safe to be authentic and vulnerable to whatever level the facilitator models this for them.
- Please note that if you are in the midst of a major personal sin or inner healing issue, this is not the place for you to share everything you are going through with a large group.

Suggestions for Timing: If you have...

- **15 minutes** - Do one lesson.
- **20-30 minutes** - Do two lessons or do one lesson and then take time to have people share what they learned with the group and pray for one another.
- **45-60 minutes** - Go over "The Kingdom of God in the Garden of Eden" (p. 2), "Are You Living in the Kingdom of God?" (p. 3), and "Getting Started" (pp.11-12), then do 2-4 lessons.
- **2 hours** - Go over the sections listed above and go through 5-8 lessons.
- **4 or more hours** - Go over the sections listed above or the whole Introduction. Do an entire chapter, or go through lessons from a variety of chapters in the book.

Types of Groups to Facilitate:
- **Daily** - Do one lesson each day, as a devotional. This can be by yourself or in a group.
- **Weekly, Every Other Week, or Monthly Small Groups** - Meet for 30 minutes to 3 hours.
- **Monthly Training Events** - Meet for a couple of hours for a bigger training event. Consider adding music and worship time as well as advertising and inviting lots of people to come.
- **Special Events** - Pick a topic you like, and get people together one time to learn about that.
- **Outreach** - Consider planning a time for your group to go out and share the Gospel, heal the sick, prophesy, and practice other activations in this manual.
- **School Plants** - Gather others who commit to each purchase and go through the entire Kingdom Culture Core book together. For more information on school plants go to KristenDarpa.com.

Teachers:
- Gather other teachers together once a week for 30 minutes or more. Do a lesson together, and share with one another what you got out of it.
- Share what is going on in your classrooms. Pray for one another and for your students.
- Do one lesson in your classroom each week. You can do this all at once in 15-30 minutes. Or, you can take 5-10 minutes each day and break the lesson down throughout a week. Monday: Topic and Bible Verses. Tuesday: Description. Wednesday and Thursday: Activations. Friday: Application. Depending upon how much time you have, you can have your students share the activation with a partner, or have some share with the entire class. You could even get an additional copyright license and send home a copy of the page with the kids each week, encouraging their families to do the lesson together.

Students:
- Gather other kids together, before or after school, once a week. Ask your teacher or principal if there is a place where you can meet at the school.
- Get kids in your neighborhood together, in your home or at a park, once a week.
- Ask your pastor or youth leader if you can use this book in your youth group, or if you can help lead a youth or kids' study in your church.
- Have kids go around and say their names to introduce themselves before starting to lead a lesson.

Pastors and Leaders:
- Use a lesson as a starting place for a sermon.
  - Have your people do an activation in church and practice what they just learned.
  - Challenge your people to activate the lesson in their daily lives during the week and come back to church with a testimony to share next week.
- Use the material to disciple new believers in small groups.
- Do a small group for anyone with this material. Empower others to facilitate.
- Use this for your youth and/or children's ministry.

Parents:
- Go through a lesson each week with your family.
- Have each person share the activation with the whole group.
- Empower other members of your family to read and facilitate a lesson.
- Talk about one of the lessons at the dinner table, before bed, or as a family devotional over breakfast/first thing in the morning.

Setting Up Your Kingdom Culture Group

Kingdom Culture groups are powerful times to connect with the Lord, His Word, and other believers. Organizing your group will help you and the others in it get as much out of your time as possible. Your group could be anything from you and one other person to a handful of friends or even a large group. Here are some basic elements to consider. Trust that the Holy Spirit will lead you as you go. You can use this same format for setting up other types of groups as well. Think through the questions below and fill in the answers in the space provided.

Place & Time: Pick a place and time to meet. It is best if this can stay the same place and time. Let people know how long you will meet (e.g. one hour, two hours, three hours, etc.). If you want to meet at your workplace or school, please make sure to get permission from your supervisor or teacher.

Where, when, and for how long will you meet? Is there anyone you need permission from?

How often will you meet (weekly, biweekly)**?**

What date will you start? Will you have an end date?

What lessons will you cover? Use the Top Lessons lists for help.

People: Who will you invite to your group? Is everyone invited or do you want to focus on a certain age, gender, etc. (e.g. moms, teenage boys, families, etc.)?

Roles: You can lead this on your own, or make it a group effort. Would you like to have other people help you facilitate? Would you like to have any other roles for the group like someone to lead worship, help with set up, etc.?

Invite: How will you let people know about your group? (Social media, email, posters, handouts, word of mouth, etc.) However you invite people, personal invitations work best.

Misc.: Do you want to have worship (live or recorded), provide snacks, offer child care, have name tags, etc.? Will you need to do any special set up? Do people need to bring anything? Can people come and go each time you meet or do you want people to commit to come for a certain amount of time?

Possible Kingdom Culture Group Structure

Depending on how long you want to meet you can plan to meet from anywhere between thirty minutes to three hours, or even longer. If you do the shortest time on all the non-optional items below, it will take you one hour. If you do the maximum time on all the items, including optional ones, it will take you three and a half hours. Please adjust times and the order of these areas as needed. Do not feel that you have to cover every area. Feel free to add in other elements like having a meal together or taking communion.

Set Up: 10 - 30 Minutes Before
Plan to have the room and any supplies set up before people arrive. If you want, you can spend some time in prayer before the group starts. Even if you do not need to set up, plan to arrive at least a few minutes early in case some people arrive ahead of time.

Settle In: 5 - 15 Minutes
Allow people time to arrive and get settled in. Depending on your schedule, you can wait for people to arrive before you start or you can start on time and remind people who are late to please come earlier.

Welcome, Overview, and Ground Rules: 5-10 Minutes
Welcome everyone and give them an overview of what you will be doing so they know what to expect. (E.g. "Tonight we will be going over lessons and activations on healing.") Read the "Getting Started" section on pages 11-12. If you have more time, especially for your first group, consider reading through pages 2, 3, and the top of 4 about the Kingdom of God and the Garden of Eden.

> **Share Testimonies:** (Optional) 5 - 10 Minutes
> What good things did God do in your life this week? How did you get to activate what you learned in group last time we met and what did you see God do as you stepped out?
>
> **IceBreaker:** (Optional) 5 Minutes (Depending on the group size)
> Icebreakers are simple questions that people answer to help get to know one another better. Even if you already all know each other, they can still be a lot of fun and help people feel comfortable. Keep people on track so this doesn't take up all of your time. You can do this while you practice switching partners. <u>Examples</u>: What was the best part of your week or what is your favorite candy, movie, etc.?
>
> **Worship:** (Optional) 5 - 20 Minutes
> In a small group setting it is good to pick one to three songs that most people would know and be able to sing without seeing words. You can use live or recorded music.

Lessons and Activations: 30 - 90 Minutes
Dive into the lessons and activations. If you are starting a new section, take the time to read the section overview. If your group is getting a lot out of an activation you can spend more time there. You are also free to spend less time on certain lessons or pick and choose which activations from the lesson you want to do.

> **Homework:** (Optional) 5 Minutes
> If you want, you can give your group one thing to work on until you meet again. (E.g. Pray for one sick person, read the Bible three times this week, etc.)

Prayer: 5 - 15 Minutes
Depending on your time limit you can either close in prayer, have people pair up with a partner or in small groups to pray together, or take time to share requests and pray together as a big group. Make sure you pray out loud together before you dismiss. Spend more time praying than you do sharing prayer requests. You can also ask people to pray out their requests instead of sharing them first.

Shorter Course Options

If you want to pick and choose lessons from throughout the book and are wondering where to start, you can use these lists of our top 20, 30, and 50 lessons.

Our Top 20 Lessons

1.	God is Good	14
2.	Loved, and Loving	17
3.	My Old Self is Gone, and I am New	19
4.	Adopted Into the Family	20
5.	Be	22
6.	On Earth as it is in Heaven	32
7.	The Power of the Testimony	34
8.	The Light is Green Unless It's Red	40
9.	Connecting with the Bible (SOAP)	43
10.	Release and Receive	62
11.	How Can I Pray for You?	68
12.	Feeling God's Presence	69
13.	Your Salvation Testimony	70
14.	Sharing the Gospel	72
15.	Five Step Healing Model	90
16.	Strengthen, Encourage, and Comfort	95
17.	Name-Based Prophecies	96
18.	Image-Based Prophecies	97
19	Adam and Eve: Having Dominion	114
20.	Change the World, Start at Home	125

Our Top 30 Lessons

1.	God is Good	14
2.	Loved, and Loving	17
3.	Connecting with the Lord	18
4.	My Old Self is Gone, and I am New	19
5.	Adopted Into the Family	20
6.	Be	22
7.	Rest	29
8.	Ministering the Presence of the Lord	30
9.	On Earth as it is in Heaven	32
10	The Power of the Testimony	34
11.	The Light is Green Unless It's Red	40
12.	Connecting with the Bible (SOAP)	43
13.	Forgiveness	60
14.	Release and Receive	62
15.	How Can I Pray for You?	68
16.	Feeling God's Presence	69
17.	Your Salvation Testimony	70
18.	Sharing the Gospel	72
19	Prayer For Salvation	74
20.	Holy Spirit Baptism	84
21.	Five Step Healing Model	90
21.	Strengthen, Encourage, and Comfort	95
23.	Name-Based Prophecies	96
24.	Image-Based Prophecies	97
25.	Rapid Fire Prophecy	100
26.	Creative Identity	110
27.	Adam and Eve: Having Dominion	114
28.	Prayer Evangelism	119
29.	Equipped and Equipping	124
30.	Change the World, Start at Home	125

Our Top 50 Lessons

1. God is Good — 14
2. Made in God's Image — 16
3. Loved, and Loving — 17
4. Connecting with the Lord — 18
5. My Old Self is Gone, and I am New — 19
6. Adopted Into the Family — 20
7. Be — 22
8. Honor — 25
9. Connection in Relationships — 27
10. Generational Thinking — 28
11. Rest — 29
12. Ministering the Presence of the Lord — 30
13. Impartation — 31
14. On Earth as it is in Heaven — 32
15. Declarations — 33
16. The Power of the Testimony — 34
17. Peace Beyond Understanding — 36
18. Strengthen Yourself in the Lord — 37
19. Jesus is the Most Normal Christian… — 39
20. The Light is Green Unless It's Red — 40
21. Relationship with the Author — 42
21. Connecting with the Bible — 43
23. Communion — 56
24. Forgiveness — 60
25. Release and Receive — 62
26. Finding the Root — 63
27. Healthy Living — 64
28. Connect — 67
29. How Can I Pray for You? — 68
30. Feeling God's Presence — 69
31. Your Salvation Testimony — 70
32. Sharing the Gospel — 72
33. Prayer For Salvation — 74
34. Treasure Hunts — 80
35. Holy Spirit Baptism — 84
36. Five Step Healing Model — 90
37. Strengthen, Encourage, and Comfort — 95
38. Name-Based Prophecies — 96
39. Image-Based Prophecies — 97
40. It's All About Love — 98
41. Processing Prophecy — 99
42. Rapid Fire Prophecy — 100
43. Creative Identity — 110
44. Adam and Eve: Having Dominion — 114
45. Joseph — 116
46. Solomon — 117
47. Seven Mountains — 118
48. Prayer Evangelism — 119
49. Equipped and Equipping — 124
50. Change the World, Start at Home — 125

Ministry Tunnel 101

Ministry tunnels are a powerful, empowering, practical way to minister to a lot of people very quickly. The ministry team forms two lines, with each person standing side by side, facing the other line. People receive ministry by walking through the center of these two lines. As they do, the ministry team members place their hands on each person's shoulder as they walk by. Ministers can speak brief declarations or one word prophecies. They can also minister impartation. These types of ministry tunnels are sometimes also called "fire," "prayer," "blessing," "glory," "prophecy," or "impartation" tunnels. Use whatever name best describes your tunnel.

Gather people you trust to minister to others. Have them form two lines, each facing the other, at the front of the room. The ministry team lines should be about an arm's length apart, with the members facing inward, standing shoulder-to-shoulder next to one another. Have them rest in the Lord's presence and then begin to minister to one another for a moment. In doing this, they will become aware of the Lord's presence and start getting comfortable ministering to others in this setting.

Instruct those walking through the tunnel and those ministering to people that this type of ministry is ministry on the move. People will walk through the tunnel and keep walking until they reach the end. They should NOT stop or "park" in the tunnel. If they fall down you can—as kindly as possible—drag them off to the side. This is NOT a time for your ministry team to give long prophetic words or do a lot of ministry or prayer. They should trust that the Lord is ministering powerfully in this time, and release a maximum of one or two words over each person as they walk by. If people do stop, have ministers gently pull or nudge them forward. If a minister does spend a long time ministering, ask them to kindly keep it moving, or pull them out of the tunnel if necessary. It can be helpful to have one main ministry leader on a microphone to direct the ministry team.

Instruct people before they go into the tunnel whether they can go back through after they have finished. If you feel confident to release all attendees to minister, you can also tell them they are welcome to join the end of the ministry lines afterward to minister to the people behind them.

Those ministering can put their hands on people's shoulders, or possibly their heads (if it is culturally appropriate), but should not put their hands on stomachs or anywhere else.

Play upbeat, lively worship music as people walk through to set the atmosphere. Make sure you have cleared away chairs and made plenty of space for the line to wrap around the room, wherever it may go.

Additional Information

This section tells the story behind how the school started and shares additional resources related to Kingdom Culture.

How It All Began

I believe a modern day mission movement is being released on the earth today that is about identity, responsibility, and creativity. All doing comes from being. All authority comes from taking responsibility. Creativity is the embodiment of the Spirit of wisdom (knowing what to do), and it actually creates new possibilities. If each of us would simply be our authentic selves (identity), take responsibility for our own lives right where we are, and go forward with kingdom creativity, then whether we go to a neighbor (local) or a nation (global) we will see transformation. I call this, "i Go Glocal." We each can be who we are, where we are. Then, whether we go to a neighbor or a nation, the result will be transformation. This is what I am going to do. I am going Glocal and I invite you to do the same!

After experiencing models like Randy Clark's Youth Power Invasion in Brazil and traveling with ministry teams with Bethel, The House, and my own ministry, I dreamed with the Lord about creating a mobile ministry school that could teach, activate, and release people into the core concepts of the kingdom. I wanted to practically equip and empower people to be their authentic selves so they could go change the world. It was all a great idea, but I needed a place to try it out.

After years of dreaming of writing a manual like this, I was encouraged by my pastor, Jamey VanGelder, to host a regular ministry training time at our church. It was his spark of encouragement that actually got me started. In 2015, I began hosting a monthly event with a number of people from our church, developing handouts for each session. I was so excited that I think everyone received about twenty pages of notes for their first class!

Later that year, my pastor graciously let me host a three day conference at our church, and I promised everyone that they would receive a manual when they came. That conference gave me the opportunity to write the majority of the expanded manual. (Interestingly enough, most of it was written and compiled over one week.) My dad and I stayed in our church's copy room for over twelve hours, printing and assembling copies. My mom helped edit, and my faithful ministry team helped punch and collate thousands of pages into binders. That week individuals, families, and leaders from around our state and surrounding areas came to our very first Kingdom Culture School (see our first graduating class below). Many of the graduates then joined my ministry team, and I led them on a month-long local mission trip around our state. Within a week after school, students started leading people to Jesus, and a steady stream of testimonies began to trickle in of the fruit of changed lives.

Broken Knee Cap Healed

Doctors told one of our nine-year-old students that she had a broken knee cap. For several weeks she had been using crutches and wearing a leg brace. She was in constant pain. During one of our sessions, Jesus told her, "I'm healing your knee." As she put it, "It got all buzzy and warm." No one even prayed for her, yet by the end of the night she was sprinting around the church!

Ears Opened

The girl who was healed had a ten-year-old brother with 80% hearing loss in one ear. After receiving prayer, he went to school the next day with a note from his father informing his teachers that he no longer needed to wear the school-provided hearing aid. While at school, he was able to share about his healing with his teacher, the school nurse, and the superintendent who was visiting that day.

Their parents were also physically healed. Then the whole family traveled the state, doing ministry with us for the rest of the month.

The Journey Continues

I spent the next year gradually editing and adding to the manual. I ran it by everyone from mega-church pastors to home-schooling moms, curriculum writers, business owners, book authors, and third-world missionaries. I did my first international school later that fall, with participants from over five African language groups. After encouragement from many different people, I decided in 2016 that it was time to start publishing books. Since then I have personally shared the *Kingdom Culture School of Ministry* around my home state of Minnesota, the United States, Mexico, Brazil, the Philippines, Liberia, Togo, and more!

Brazil

After seeing children powerfully impacted by a school at Eden Church in Pillager, Minnesota, I started dreaming with a Brazilian friend about taking *Kingdom Culture* to her nation, where she runs a pre-school for children of drug dealers and teaches 3rd grade in a public school run by a witch. These schools are located in a community surrounded by a drug war. We asked the public school principal to please give us her school for one week to run a ministry school…and she thought that was a great idea! Every morning we ran an interactive ministry school for 3-5th graders, in the afternoon we ran one for the preschoolers, and each evening we ran one for adults.

Additional Information - 139

Two boys in the public school drew pictures of how God saw the other boy and then embraced each other. Their teacher later told me that each boy had family members who were murdered by members of the other boy's family.

One day when the public school kids were out of control, we began to worship. They settled down, and many began to encounter the love of the Lord. The rest of the school heard about this and wanted to be a part of it, so the next day we gathered them all for a short time of worship. Two songs turned into ninety minutes! Kids started seeing heaven and angels. Then kids started praying for teachers, and teachers for their students. Several teachers were healed, and the principal was also powerfully touched.

Language Translations
The *Kingdom Culture School of Ministry* is currently available in English, Spanish, Portuguese, Polish, Russian, French and Indonesian. More translations are coming soon!

My dream is for the body of Christ around the world to be empowered, equipped, trained, and activated into the fullness of her identity and destiny. I believe the transformation of society will happen through normal, everyday believers like you and me. Someday I hope to see a movement of mobile ministry schools sent out everywhere from the mountains of influence to the lowest, the least, and the lost.

This is the story of how the school and manuals began. Where it will go is a journey still unfolding. As we go forward, I would love to hear your testimonies and feedback about what God has done in your life through this material. Let us continue to see mindsets shifted and culture transformed through biblically based, experiential learning. Thank you so much for purchasing this book and for being willing to embrace all that heaven has, both for you and for the world around you!

Blessings, Joy, and Peace,

- Kristen D'Arpa

KristenDArpa.com
Facebook.com/KristenDArpa.iGG

Acknowledgements

Mom and Dad, thank you so much for all you have done to believe in me and this work! Thank you for sending me to all of the places where I received this information. Thank you for telling me to dream big and that, someday, I would write a book. Thank you for giving me a nest to launch from and wings to soar! You've spent countless hours helping me make copies, editing, coming to ALL of my classes, and praying to see me through. All things considered, this project would most certainly not have happened without you!

Pastors Jamey and Nicole VanGelder, thank you for bringing me into The House family, loving me, believing in me, and giving me so many opportunities to learn and grow—not only in ministry, but also as a child of God. The atmosphere and culture you've created at The House is like no other place in the world, and it was from this place and family that these materials were birthed. Thank you also for allowing me to be a part of The House School of Ministry and letting me speak into and be a part of the lives of our precious students. Thank you for letting me teach this class as one of our small groups, and for opening up our space to do my first real conference/school. You've truly changed my life in more ways than I can count, and I look forward to journeying together with you for many years to come. May you receive much inheritance from the fruit that these books bring.

Thank you Pastor Bill Johnson, Kris Vallotton, Steve Backlund, Danny Silk, Heidi Baker, and so many other staff members of Bethel Church. I am forever grateful for the three years I spent growing in and hatching from the cocoons of Bethel and Iris. The entire concept of "activation" exploded in my life when I met and interned with Theresa Dedmon. "Mama T" taught me that I could run farther and faster than I ever knew possible—and also gave me many life lessons for how to run strong and steady for the long haul. Thanks for being a trusted mentor and dear friend.

Diana Kokku, thank you for your incredible friendship and sisterhood on this journey! Thank you for all of the hours of moral support, encouragement, media assistance, strategic planning, and dreaming. This project would not have happened without you.

Princeton Kokku, thank you for all of your support and encouragement over the years, and for always adding strength to my journey.

Nathalie Benson, thank you for your precious and faithful friendship. Thank you for running with me and encouraging me to stay the course as these materials were birthed and brought forth.

Del and Katie Lafky, watch lions and dear friends. Thanks for telling me to go for it, that I'm good, and that I would surely produce something great if I listened to my heart.

Dave and Noreen Hauer, thank you for championing my cause, for your consistent care, for reminding me to enjoy the present, and for stirring up my heart towards the nations. Thanks for keeping me grounded and reminding me to keep running.

Roger and Myrna, thank you for helping to pioneer our translations and for getting this book to Eastern Europe, the land for whom it was originally written.

Midge, thank you for coming on to help with editing and translation formatting and for being such a faithful friend and running mate all these years!

Carole Smith, thank you for tirelessly editing all the updates and to you and Jim for journeying with me around the world.

Kathy Silvers, thank you for imparting to the book process and for taking this to nations.

Angela Smith, thank you for working with all of our interpreters and for being the bridge to get the books out to the world.

Pam and Anne, thank you for believing in me, encouraging me over tea, and inspiring me to live a beautiful life. Pam, thanks for reminding me of who I am and the place I have at Bethel. Anne, thank you for your encouragement to get this work published and for bringing a copy to the Middle East.

Janene and Esther, thank you for pioneering this school with me and for standing alongside me and our Circuit Rider MN ministry team. Watching you both teach from this material was a great encouragement to me.

Circuit Riders MN team of 2015, thank you for being a part of our first schools, and for all of you who punched and collated thousands of pages.

Margaret Fischer, you are super woman of missions, all things editing, hot pot buffets, and a great friend. THANK YOU for all of your edits, your insights, and your eye for excellence.

Coreene Lubeley, thank you for jumping in to edit at the last minute, and for helping me stay healthy in the final push to get this out.

David Sluka, thank you for validating this project and for giving me immensely valuable advice at very key moments along the way.

Dana and Kathy D'Arpa, thanks for being such a supportive brother and sister-in-law, and for praying for and encouraging me in this process. Kathy, thanks for taking time to read through my book, and for telling me you'd take my class. Dana, thank you for your prayers and love throughout all of this, and for teaching me so much about the Bible.

Dawn, thank you for all of your graphic design and logo work over the years, for your heart-felt support, and for always making everything look so incredibly good.

Kelli, Jodi, Dawn, Myrna, Theresa, Marsha, Nicole, Karis, and everyone else who took an entire weekend to read through every word and give feedback, thank you! Thank you to Charleson Meadows for hosting our feedback weekend.

John and Amy, thank you for your constant support and friendship, and for writing your first endorsement.

Em, thanks for hosting me in Brazil and for having the courage to let me take your public school kids through a ministry school.

And to all the countless others who have been involved, thank you!

All My Love and Appreciation,
- Kristen D'Arpa

Kingdom Culture School Resources

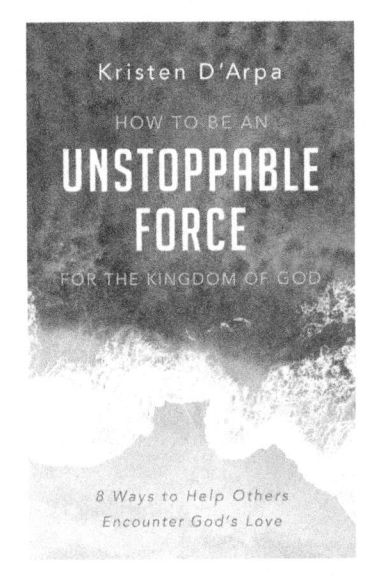

Kingdom Culture: How to Be an Unstoppable Force
Contains eight principles that will make you an unstoppable force for the kingdom of God. This small booklet also contains stories and testimonies about each principle.

Topics Include: Connection, Prayer, Prophecy, Healing, Testimonies, the Gospel, Journey, and Adjusting.

Time to Complete: 5 - 8 hours, in a group setting.

Kingdom Culture School of Ministry: Core
Contains 80 kingdom concepts and 180 activations bringing a year's worth of ministry school experience into one hand-held reference.

Topics Include: Identity, Kingdom Mindsets, the Bible, Foundational Principles, Personal Health, Outreach, Spiritual Gifts, Physical Healing, Prophecy, Kingdom Creativity, and Societal Transformation.

Time to Complete: 25-40 hours, in a group setting.

Kingdom Culture School of Ministry: Expanded Contains over 250 kingdom concepts and 340 activations in every area of kingdom living.

Topics Include: Kingdom Concepts Throughout Biblical History, Kingdom Mindsets, Foundational Principles, Bible Study, Personal Health, Outreach, Spiritual Gifts, Physical Healing, Prophecy, Kingdom Creativity, Societal Transformation, and The New Heavens and New Earth.

Time to Complete: 100 hours to two months, in a group setting. Also great as an ongoing resource.

To order manuals or request a live-taught school in your area, visit:
KristenDArpa.com

Additional Languages Available

Books are currently available in Spanish, Portuguese, Polish, Russian, French, and Indonesian. More translations are coming soon! Contact us about additional language translations.

Other Books by Kristen D'Arpa

Photo Stories: Encouraging and Uplifting Prophetic Photographs This pocket-sized outreach tool contains 92 removable pictures of original artwork or global missions snapshots. Go online to read the story of each photo, and share the story of what happened when you gave that photo away! Includes outreach testimonies and instruction guide.

The Pull Spark conversation with this coffee table book of photography, artwork, poetry, and God encounters.

Spiritual Dim Sum This interactive coffee table book is brimming with testimonies, short stories, vibrant photos and artwork, and creative writing based upon what the Lord is doing around the world today.

Contact Us

Contact our team if you would like to bring a live-taught school to your area or would like to help with a language translation.

KristenDArpa.com

Made in the USA
Coppell, TX
28 August 2021